The Tony Award®

A COMPLETE LISTING OF WINNERS AND NOMINEES OF THE AMERICAN THEATRE WING'S TONY AWARD

With a History of the American Theatre Wing

Edited by
ISABELLE STEVENSON
and
ROY A. SOMLYO

HEINEMANN
Portsmouth, New Hampshire

Heinemann
A division of Reed Elsevier Inc.
361 Hanover Street
Portsmouth, NH 03801–3912
www.heinemanndrama.com

Offices and agents throughout the world

The Cataloging-in-Publication Data is on file with the Library of Congress.
ISBN 0-325-00294-0

Editor: Lisa A. Barnett
Production editor: Sonja S. Chapman
Cover design: Jenny Jensen Greenleaf
Manufacturing: Deanna Richardson

Printed in the United States of America on acid-free paper
05 04 03 02 01   DA   1 2 3 4 5

Contents

Contents

List of Photographs

Preface

Since the inception of the Antoinette Perry Awards in 1947, the selection of categories by Tony Awards® Administration Committees has undergone many changes. The categories have, from season to season, been redefined, added to, and subtracted from, in order to remain flexible and to accommodate the ever-changing Broadway theatrical scene.

The governing principle and yardstick for selecting a particular play, actor, etc., has, from the very beginning, been "distinguished achievement in the theatre" rather than "best." Therefore, on several occasions the committee has selected two or three winners in the same category. For example, José Ferrer and Fredric March both won in the category of dramatic actor in 1947; *Fiorello!* and *The Sound of Music* both received Tonys in the musical category in 1960; Anna Maria Alberghetti and Diahann Carroll both received awards in the leading actress in a musical category in 1962; John Lee Beatty and David Mitchell both won in the scenic design category in 1980; and *Kiss of the Spider Woman—The Musical* and *The Who's Tommy* tied in 1993 in the score category.

Until 1956, the selection of winners was announced, but the nominees were not. Therefore, during these first years (1947-1955) no list of nominees is available. Since 1956, the American Theatre Wing's Tony® nominations have been publicly announced in each category.

Certain categories were added over the years. For example, the first award for lighting design was given in 1970, and the orchestration category was added in 1998. A star denotes the winner in each category.

The Special Awards presented each year are given for many reasons. For example, Helen Menken's presentation to Gilbert Miller for his distinguished career as producer in the theatre; Cary Grant's tribute to Noel Coward for his contribution to the American theatre; and presentations to many others for their loyal and interested support of the theatre.

Special Awards have also been given to such shows as *Good Evening* and A *Thurber Carnival* which fit into no specific category but which merited recognition for excellence. Commencing in 2001, a new category addresses this achievement annually.

Many of the Wing's illustrious and dedicated volunteers have also received Special Awards for their devotion to the Wing's mission. An award was given posthumously to Helen Menken for her years of devoted service to the Wing as president and member of the board. Rosamond Gilder, Vera Allen, and Mrs. Martin Beck also received awards for their dedication and service. In 1999, Isabelle Stevenson, then chairman of the Wing, was awarded a Special Tony for Lifetime Achievement.

History of the American Theatre Wing

"It would be wonderful to keep alive this great spirit of unity which has held the men and women of the theatre together—that if we are ever needed again in a call which must supersede everything else in the world, we are here and ready—and if it comes after we ourselves are gone, we shall leave it in the annals of the theatre that the trained imagination of the theatre can be used for serving humanity in more ways than entertaining, and that when it is called it leaps unafraid into the saddle and rides fast and far and to the end."

— Rachel Crothers
Founder and President,
American Theatre Wing
Theatre Arts, April 1941

THE STAGE IS SET—THE CAST ASSEMBLES

If a Tony is ever given to the longest-running service organization in the theatre, it should go to the American Theatre Wing. On the eve of America's entry into the first World War in 1917, seven ladies of theatre—Rachel Crothers, Louise Closser Hale, Dorothy Donnelly, Josephine Hull, Minnie Dupree, Bessie Tyree, and Louise Drew—converged to discuss the possibility of forming an organization to aid in war relief. At the meeting, these ladies decided to summon members of the theatre world together to determine how to contribute to the war effort. Two weeks later people representing every segment of the family of theatre—from the internationally famous to wardrobe mistresses, stagehands, and producers—packed the Hudson Theatre to its doors. The Stage Women's War Relief was born and began operation within the next few weeks. The organization established workrooms for sewing, with output totaling 1,863,645 articles; clothing and food collection centers; a canteen on Broadway for servicemen; and began sending troops of entertainers to perform wherever needed. Perhaps most significantly, speakers, trained by the organization, sold Liberty Bonds. As Rachel Crothers stated in her report on the activities of the Stage Women's War Relief during the Great War, "Whereas The Stage Women's War Relief amassed for its own disbursement $241,602.72—for other War Reliefs and for our country we raised the sum of $6,996,678.87." Through the vision and patriotism of the theatre community, the Stage Women's War Relief became one of the most significant and active relief organizations in the world.

Although the need for relief activities diminished after the Treaty of Versailles in 1919, Ms. Crothers and her comrades continued their activities. In 1920, theatre men formed a brother committee to work with the women on behalf of the civilian population still recovering from the hardships of the war.

In 1939, the United States government asked Rachel Crothers to reactivate her committee. In January 1940, Ms. Crothers along with Josephine Hull, Minnie Dupree, Antoinette Perry, Vera Allen, Gertrude Lawrence, Lucile Watson, Theresa Helburn, and Edith Atwater formed the American Theatre Wing under the auspices of the "Allied Relief Fund." Later the Allied Fund merged with the British War Relief Society. During the two years before the United States entered the Second World War, the American Theatre Wing gave $81,760.45 in civilian aid to Britain, including more than $40,000 raised in a benefit staged by Gilbert Miller, chairman of the men's division.

During this time, many of the theatre's most distinguished performers worked far away from the footlights. Minutes from a June 4, 1940 meeting show that the workroom committee headed by Lucile Watson included Peggy Conklin, Ruth Gordon, Uta Hagen, and Vivian Vance. Crothers stated of these efforts: "There is no *glamour* in this workroom but a great deal of *glory*—because of its steadfast marching growth—the result of long hours of hard work."

After the attack on Pearl Harbor on December 7, 1941, the Wing became an independent organization. The charter states: "To render voluntary service and aid toward the successful prosecution by the United States of the war in which it is now engaged . . . It is primarily a War Service Corporation with emphasis on the service functions and features of such work." Forty-three members—a "Who's Who" of the theatre—comprised the executive board. Rachel Crothers served as president; Gertrude Lawrence, Helen Hayes, and Vera Allen served as vice-presidents; and Josephine Hull was treasurer. Antoinette Perry served as both chairman of the board and secretary.

The men's executive committee included Gilbert Miller, Brooks Atkinson, George S. Kaufman, Raymond Massey, Brock Pemberton, Billy Rose, Lee Shubert, Max Gordon, and Vinton Freedley.

After the United States entered the war, the Hudson Theatre again served as the scene for a mass meeting of the entertainment industry; many of the Wing's most famous and effective activities, including the legendary Stage Door Canteens, resulted from these efforts. Eight Stage Door Canteens throughout the United States, as well as in London and Paris, served soldiers. In New York, Jane Cowl and Selena Royle served as the co-chairs of the Canteen. Opened on March 2, 1942 in the 44th Street Theatre, donated by Lee Shubert, the New York Stage Door Canteen serviced an average of 3,000 servicemen a night. In an average night, according to Marian Moore, the co-chair of food preparation, the Canteen served: 2,000 sandwiches, 3,000 slices of cake or doughnuts, 1,000 half pints of milk, 80 gallons of fruit juice and cider, 25 lbs. of candy, six crates of fruit, and 5,000 cigarettes. Theatrical luminaries gave of their time and talents in the Canteens. Katharine Cornell gladly cleaned off tables, Marlene Dietrich frequently assisted at the milk bar, Radie Harris brought in talent to work at the Canteen, Jean Dalrymple chaired the publicity committee, and lyricist Dorothy Fields became a master at washing pots and pans. Alfred Lunt, who was considered a master chef, refused to cook. "Put me on garbage," he requested.

"The garbage?" gasped his stricken colleagues, "why the garbage?"

"Because I want to see what they're not eating," he replied, "and then we can adjust the menus."

In 1971, actress Paula Laurence reminisced about life in the Canteen: "Those of us who could entertain the troops, did; those who couldn't, danced with the servicemen, waited on tables, or washed dishes with considerably more skill than the high-priced help which served us at home. We were all performing a needed service and vice-versa, for all these activities were wondrously therapeutic in relieving the guilts we all suffered because our lives were comparatively undisturbed; we weren't flying bombers or being shipped to crematoriums."

Providing a magical escape from the war, the Stage Door Canteens served both a moral and a spiritual duty—enabling soldiers and civilians to joyously remember a time of peace and to look forward to the day when the forces of justice would again triumph.

Although the famous Stage Door Canteens provide the fodder by which legends grow, the Wing's reach extended well beyond 44th Street. At the height of the war, the Wing sponsored fifty-four separate programs—in New York and around the world—any one of which ranked as a major war service. With the money earned from the movie *Stage Door Canteen*, the Wing gave $75,000 to the USO to inaugurate legitimate drama as entertainment for soldiers overseas. Katharine Cornell, the veritable actress of such dark beauty, starred in the first play, The Barretts of Wimpole Street.

The Victory Players, which also produced legitimate theatre, enlightened and inspired civilians on the home front with its plays teaching families how to deal emotionally, and pragmatically with their loved ones returning from war. From February 1942 through October 1945, the Victory Players gave 1,004 performances in the New York area comprising 4,451 individual performances by actors. The Victory Players even performed to an audience estimated at 100,000 in Central Park.

The weekly radio program "Stage Door Canteen" raised income and just as in the Great War, the Wing trained speakers to sell bonds. The "Lunchtime Follies", a series of revues, entertained workers in defense plants, although lunch often occurred at midnight.

Wartime also saw the launch of the Hospital Entertainment program, which still prospers today. Esther Hawley, who later won a Special Tony Award, organized the hospital committee in 1943. Vera Allen, Ben Grauer, Elaine Perry, and Russel Crouse are but a few who were active on the hospital committee. In total, during World War II and the first eight months after, the Wing sent out nearly 6,700 ward units. At the Wing's peak the hospital program served 25 hospitals within a radius of 75 miles of New York. The Wing sent out about 1,200 entertainers each month. During the same period, flying with the Naval Air Corps, the Wing sent units to ten Naval and Marine hospitals. In all, the Navy flew in 97 units, including plays, using 617 people, for weekend hospital performances.

During the first postwar year, the Hospital Program still sent out 650 people a month. Branches of the Wing in Washington, D.C. and Boston had equally impressive records.

When the war ended, the Wing turned its attention to the returning veteran. On September 13, 1945, a letter went to all members calling for the first meeting of the planning committee for postwar activities. The committee met the following week, and soon the Wing adapted its programs to fill the needs of postwar America. The Wing's two lofty purposes—to further the welfare of the theatre itself and to utilize the resources of the theatre in the service of the community—remained at the forefront of the Wing's actions and undertakings. The changes at the Wing mirrored the changes of the Allied Powers, as victory brought a renewed focus on life at home. For those families beginning to face the homecoming of wounded and the problems brought on by separation, the Wing changed the name of the Victory Players to the Community Players. The Community Players commissioned plays for such organizations as the National Conference of Christians and Jews, the American Red Cross and the National Association for Mental Health. These half-hour sketches focused on many problems plaguing domestic society—poverty, cancer, safety, race relations, and mental health. Written by outstanding American playwrights, these plays served as catalysts for family discussion. Katharine Cornell and Mrs. Henry N. Pratt led the Community Players as co-chairwomen, and Vera Allen, Mrs. Paul Raymer, and Cornelia Otis Skinner served as vice-chairwomen. In 1958, the Community Players were rechristened Plays for Living.

In the spring of 1947, the Wing took another dramatic step. A specialized recreation program was launched, and the teaching of its technique to staff and volunteer workers in each of the neuropsychiatric hospitals under the Veterans Administration was started. Teams of Wing actresses, selected for their experience and particular qualities, resigned their theatre and radio jobs for a three-and-a-half month tour.

The Wing also dedicated itself to educating those who served the Allied Powers during the war and put into motion a plan to build a theatre school for the returning veteran. Founded by Vera Allen, Mary Hunter, and Winston O'Keefe, the American Theatre Wing Professional School opened its doors on July 8, 1946. Theresa Helburn, Maurice Evans, and Louis Simon were among those on the advisory committee. Mr. O'Keefe served as director, later succeeded by Mr. Simon.

School hours were 10 A.M. to midnight, and the students hailed from all areas of theatre, representing every theatrical union. The original curriculum grew from twenty-three to fifty courses offered.

To name all those who taught would be to list almost every distinguished name from theatre, television, the opera, and music. Lehman Engel, Leon Barzin, and Joseph Rosenstock taught conducting. Alfred Lunt, Eva Le Gallienne, Sir Cedric Hardwicke, Cyril Ritchard, José Ferrer, and Maureen Stapleton taught acting. Martha

Graham, Hanya Holm, José Limon, Charles Weidman, Ray Bolger, and Katherine Dunham taught dance. Kermit Bloomgarden lectured on producing and brought in fellow producers as guests. Delbert Mann and Ezra Stone headed TV workshops.

There were courses in Hebrew liturgical singing and repertoire, business and stage management, and one on music for actors and directors taught by Richard Rodgers and Oscar Hammerstein, II. John Houseman, Uta Hagen, Harold Clurman, Henry Fonda, Tennessee Williams, Alfred Drake, and Arthur Miller all gave guest lectures.

Among Wing students, all professionals, but not yet famous, were: George Burns, Richard Chamberlin, Bob Fosse, Charlton Heston, Pat Hingle, Gordon MacRae, Russell Nype, Geraldine Page, Christopher Plummer, Tony Randall, Jason Robards, Jr., William Warfield, and James Whitmore, as well as leading singers of the Met and the New York City Opera Company who came to improve their acting. Marge and Gower Champion, already a starring dance team, came to study music.

At its peak, the school enrolled 1,200 students, many of them studying on their GI Bill of Rights. The school continued to fulfill its obligation to veterans until its close in 1965. In 1951, the program opened to civilians, and in 1952, to experienced non-professionals.

Throughout the years, many of the most eminent women in the theatre community have led the Wing. Vera Allen succeeded Antoinette Perry as chairman in 1946 for one term, followed by Mrs. Martin Beck, and Helen Menken who served in that position until she became president in 1957. Helen Hayes succeeded Rachel Crothers as president in 1950, and Helen Menken followed Ms. Hayes as president in 1957. After Helen Menken's death in 1966, Isabelle Stevenson, who had been a board member since 1957, assumed the presidency. Under her leadership, the Wing's programs continued to expand. She created the "Working in the Theatre" seminars and also the Theatre-In-Schools program. In keeping with the tradition, Mrs. Stevenson had been actively engaged in the theatre and, prior to her marriage, appeared in theatres throughout the United States, Europe, and Australia. Mrs. Stevenson served as president until 1998 when she became chairman of the board and veteran Broadway producer Roy A. Somlyo took the helm as the first male president of the American Theatre Wing.

Under Mr. Somlyo's leadership, the American Theatre Wing today continues to expand its programs designed to further the highest standards of theatre. Like his predecessors, Mr. Somlyo was a theatrical professional before he became president of the Wing. He has enjoyed an active career as a producer in both theatre and television

Photo: Anita and Steve Shevett

ISABELLE STEVENSON

working with virtually every star in the entertainment world. He has been associated with the American Theatre Wing's Tony Awards since their first network telecast in 1967 and has been awarded four Emmy Awards, three as a producer of "The Tony Awards."

The Wing focuses its concern on youth. As a Rockefeller Foundation study shows, the great majority of those who attend the theatre today attended the theatre as children. By introducing young people to the theatre, the Wing educates and builds the audience that will support the theatre of tomorrow. Through the "Introduction to Broadway" program, high school students attend Broadway shows and experience the wonder of live theatre—often for the first time. With the cooperation of the producers, the New York City Board of Education, the Archdiocese of New York, and the American Theatre Wing, a minimal ticket price is established. The student pays $2.50 and the Wing pays the balance. Some of the biggest hits of the last decade, including Les Misérables, Miss Saigon, Cats, and Beauty and the Beast, have graciously opened their doors to "Introduction to Broadway" participants. Often, many of the students take part in post-show discussions with cast and crew after the performance. In its first nine years, the program sent more than 80,000 students to Broadway shows.

The Wing also touches young people with the Theatre-In-Schools program. Through this program, eminent New York theatre professionals visit New York City high schools to share their experiences with young artists. Since its inception in 1991, professionals such as actors Robert Cuccioli (Tony nominee), Marilu Henner, Karen Ziemba (Tony winner), and Edie Falco; directors Vivian Matalon (Tony winner) and Scott Elliott; playwright Warren Leight (Tony winner); and others have participated in workshops with high school students about the craft and the business. To give younger students an introduction to theatre, the Wing's newest program—the Readers' Bureau—brings Broadway personalities into elementary schools to read a short story to students. The students then write and perform a short play based on the story. The program gives children the opportunity, early in their lives, to experience the wonder of the theatrical production process. Through these programs targeted to youth, the Wing directly reaches young people in schools and helps to teach them that art has worth, meaning, and holds a world of opportunity.

In the tradition of its hospital program during the two world wars, the Wing continues to bring professional performers to entertain 30,000 people a year in hospitals, pediatric care centers, AIDS facilities, and senior citizens' centers. Through the generosity of its performers and supporters, the Wing now sponsors programs every day of the year, with over 800 total performances annually. This is the Wing's oldest program—and quite possibly the most essential.

The Wing also sponsors seminars on "Working in the Theatre." These are held in the spring and fall of each year for students, professional members of the theatrical unions, and members of the American Theatre Wing. Here, they have the opportunity to listen and talk to some of America's most distinguished actors, directors, producers, designers, and playwrights. Theatre professionals moderate these seminars which have been hosted by Isabelle Stevenson. The list of participants in these seminars includes such luminaries as: Glenn Close, Liam Neeson, Natasha Richardson, Sarah Jessica Parker, Matthew Broderick, Sandy Duncan, Mary Tyler Moore, Ann Reinking, John Malkovich, Sigourney Weaver, Marlo Thomas, Swoosie Kurtz, Blythe Danner, Frank Langella, Lynn Redgrave, Michael Crawford, John Lithgow, Kate Nelligan, Ed Asner, Madeline Kahn, Joan Allen, Vanessa Redgrave, Kathleen Turner, Jane Alexander, Stockard Channing, Richard Dreyfuss, Martin Short, David Cassidy, Mickey Rooney, Gregory Hines, Christine Baranski, Judd Hirsch, Julie Harris, Chita Rivera, Bebe Neuwirth, Valerie Harper, Nathan Lane, Nell Carter, Joel Grey, Billy Crudup, Stephen Sondheim, Angela Lansbury, Harold Prince, Tommy Tune, Brian Stokes Mitchell, Patrick Stewart, and Brian Dennehy. The seminars conclude with a period of questions from the audience. Taped at the studios of the City University of New York, the seminars are shown five times a week on CUNY-TV, on MetroGuide, and cable systems in California. The Wing distributes edited versions to schools and libraries across the country and PBS offers them to educational systems nationally.

In recent years, the Wing's scholarship programs have been expanded. Recognizing the importance of, and need for new playwrights, grants have been made to the Eugene O'Neill Theater Center, The New Dramatists, Playwrights Horizons and to as many as fifty developing theatre companies throughout New York City. The American Theatre Wing's annual scholarship programs include: American Academy of Dramatic Arts, Brendan Gill Playwright Scholarship at Talent Unlimited High School, Bernard Jacobs Scholarship at DeWitt Clinton High School, and Isabelle Stevenson Scholarships at F. H. LaGuardia High School of Music & Art and Performing Arts.

The Wing remains a not-for-profit charity, and private and corporate contributions, membership dues, fundraising efforts, and a portion of the proceeds from the annual Tony Award telecast support its programs. The idea of professional service to the community and high quality of performance exemplified by Rachel Crothers back in 1917 continues in the Wing's present activities.

The Antoinette Perry (Tony) Awards

ANTOINETTE PERRY
(1888–1946)

Actress, producer, director, chairman of the board, and secretary of the American Theatre Wing. The Tony Awards were named in her honor.

The Tony, named in honor of Antoinette Perry, remains one of the theatre's most coveted awards and is annually bestowed on professionals for "distinguished achievement" in the theatre.

When Antoinette Perry died on June 28, 1946 at the age of 58, many people who knew her were determined that she not be forgotten. As chairman of the board and secretary of the American Theatre Wing throughout World War II, Antoinette Perry insisted on perfection and high standards of quality. Her dedication and tireless efforts to broaden the scope of theatre through the many programs of the American Theatre Wing affected hundreds of people.

Born in Denver, Colorado in 1888, Antoinette Perry made her first impact on the theatre in 1906, when she was only eighteen.

She played opposite David Warfield in *Music Master* and, the follow-ing year, in David Belasco's *A Grand Army Man*. Only two years later, and at an age when most actresses are still waiting for that first big break, Antoinette Perry retired, a star, to marry and raise a family.

Following in their mother's footsteps, her daughters, Elaine and Margaret, also pursued careers in the theatre. Elaine became an active member of the American Theatre Wing as well as a the-atrical arbitrator and Broadway producer, and Margaret, who under-studied Ingrid Bergman in *Lilliom*, stage-managed the touring production of *The Barretts of Wimpole Street*.

In 1922, after the death of her husband Frank Freuauff, Antoinette Perry returned to the stage and appeared in many plays, including *Minick*, by George S. Kaufman and Edna Ferber, in 1924, and Margaret Anglin's 1927 production of *Electra*. In association with Brock Pemberton, she then turned her talent to directing, enriching the theatre with several memorable plays, including Preston Sturges' comedy *Strictly Dishonorable*, in 1929 and Mary Chase's classic, *Harvey*, in 1944. *Harvey* was a giant hit and Ms. Perry tragically died during its Broadway run.

When Antoinette Perry died, Jacob Wilk, the head of the Story Department for Warner Brothers east coast office, suggested the idea of an Antoinette Perry Memorial to John Golden. He, in turn, presented the idea to the Wing. Brock Pemberton, a long-time per-sonal friend as well as business associate, was appointed chairman of the committee, and suggested that the Wing give a series of annual awards in her name. A panel of six members was appointed to nominate candidates for the award in each category. The mem-bers who made the selections—by secret ballot—in the first year were: Vera Allen, Louise Beck, Jane Cowl, Helen Hayes, Brooks Atkinson, Kermit Bloomgarden, Clayton Collyer, George Heller, Rudy Karnolt, Burns Mantle, Gilbert Miller, Warren P. Munsell, Solly Pernick, James E. Sauter, and Oliver Sayler.

The first awards were presented at a dinner in the Grand Ballroom of the Waldorf-Astoria on Easter Sunday, April 6, 1947. With Vera Allen, Antoinette Perry's successor as Wing chairwoman, presiding, the evening included dining, dancing, and a program of entertainment whose participants included Mickey Rooney, Herb Shriner, Ethel Waters, and David Wayne. WOR radio and the Mutual Network announced the awards at midnight.

During the first two years, there was no official Tony award. The winners were presented with, in addition to a scroll, a cigarette lighter, a money clip, or a compact. The United Scenic Artists spon-sored a contest for a suitable design for the awards and Herman

Rosse's entry, depicting the masks of comedy and tragedy on one side and the profile of Antoinette Perry on the other, was selected. In 1949, the medallion was initiated at the third annual dinner. It continues to be the official Tony Award, and since 1967 has been mounted on a black base.

From 1947 until 1965, the dinner and Tony Award presentation were held in various ballrooms of such hotels as the Plaza, the Waldorf-Astoria and the Hotel Astor. The ceremonies were broadcast over WOR radio and the Mutual Network and, in 1956, televised for the first time on Du Mont's Channel 5. Brock Pemberton, Mrs. Martin Beck, Helen Hayes, and Ilka Chase presided over the ceremonies and awards presentations and entertainment was provided by Ralph Bellamy, Joan Crawford, Alfred de Liagre Jr., Gilbert Miller, Shirley Booth, Carol Channing, Joan Fontaine, Paul Newman, Geraldine Page, Anne Bancroft, Sidney Poitier, Fredric March, Robert Goulet, Gig Young, Anna Maria Alberghetti, Henry Fonda, Patricia Neal, and many others.

In 1965, Helen Menken, in failing health, announced her intention to retire from the Wing—an action that may have signaled the end for the Tony Awards. On behalf of the League of New York Theatres, Harold Prince convinced Miss Menken to withdraw her resignation. Thus the Awards continued and a partnership with the League began.

In spite of the death of Helen Menken in March of 1966, the awards were presented at the Rainbow Room the following month. The ceremony was subdued and, for the first and only time, held in the afternoon without public attendance or entertainment.

In 1967, the American Theatre Wing authorized the League of New York Theatres to present the Tony Awards when the ceremonies moved from the traditional hotel ballroom setting to a Broadway theatre at the suggestion of Alvin Cooperman, who was vice president of special programs at NBC-TV. For the first time, television viewers nationwide had the opportunity to watch the presentation of the Tony Awards. Although the Tony Awards telecast is three hours long today, the first telecast was limited to only an hour, so the program was hurried, especially toward the end. At the very end of the ceremony, Robert Preston rushed to rejoin his co-host, Mary Martin, after receiving his Tony Award for his performance in I Do! I Do! and launched into a scripted quote from Samuel Johnson. With the stage manager frantically signaling Mr. Preston to wrap things up, the new Tony winner bungled the quote. The first network telecast of the Tony Awards ended with Mary Martin turning to Robert Preston, shaking her head sadly, and taking his new Tony away from him—a fitting cap to a monumental evening.

For twenty years, Alexander H. Cohen produced the nationwide television show and organized the ball and supper dance after the awards. In 1987, the Wing formed a joint venture with the League (now the League of American Theatres and Producers) to present the awards and expand social events. That entity, Tony Award Productions, continues to manage all the aspects of the awards. The American Theatre Wing continues to preserve the original quality of intimacy by holding a party each year at Sardi's, two weeks prior to the ceremony, for Wing members and friends to salute the Tonys® and the Stage Door Canteen.

In 1996, the American Theatre Wing's Tony Awards celebrated their 50th anniversary. The following year, Radio City Music Hall served as the venue for the award presentation for the first time. A year of firsts, 1997 marked the first time the awards were broadcast on PBS for the first hour and CBS for the following two hours as well as the first time the awards were hosted by Broadway's biggest fan, Rosie O'Donnell. In 2000, after a one-year absence from Radio City Music Hall due to its renovation, the Tony Awards returned to Radio City to welcome the millennium and continue to celebrate excellence in theatre.

VOTING

In 1947, the originating committee devised a voting system whose eligible voters were members of the board of the American Theatre Wing, representing management, and the performer and craft unions of the entertainment field. In 1954, voting eligibility was expanded to include theatre professionals who were not members of the American Theatre Wing. Today the system has been further enlarged. Persons eligible to vote for winners of the Tony Awards, besides the board of directors of the American Theatre Wing and its Advisory Board, are members of the governing boards of Actors' Equity Association, the Dramatists Guild, the Society of Stage Directors and Choreographers, United Scenic Artists, and the Association of Theatrical Press Agents and Managers, those persons whose names appear on the first night press list, members of the Theatrical Council of the Casting Society of America, and certain active members of the League of American Theatres and Producers. There are approximately 700 Tony voters.

The Tony Awards Nominating Committee is a rotating group of up to thirty theatre professionals selected by the Tony Awards Administration Committee who serve for overlapping three-year terms. They are asked to see every Broadway production and then meet on the Sunday afternoon following the Tony eligibility deadline to vote on the nominations. The nominations are announced the next morning at Sardi's, the legendary theatre district eatery.

The accounting firm of Lutz & Carr supervises the entire voting and nominating process. With the sole exception of that firm's representatives, no one knows the results of the voting until they are announced on the telecast.

In 1998, the Tonys launched a Website that today, with the participation of IBM, has become the definitive site for information about the awards as well as related news and feature stories. Continually updated, the site is reachable at http://www.tonys.org.

You Want to Go on the Stage

By Antoinette Perry

You want to go on the stage. You are at the threshold of your career. What must you do to join the pageant of the theatre?

What gifts do you bring?

What lessons must you learn?

First and foremost your desire to act must be such that "many waters cannot quench nor neither can flood drown it." You must be confident of the terms of that desire. Be sure that your desire is not based on boredom, an urge for so-called freedom, or the necessity of earning a livelihood. If these be your motivations, stop where you are, retreat with dignity and be grateful that you have been warned in time to save yourself wasted years and drab, dull heartaches. Boredom with life is a native quality which makes disastrous cargo for anyone embarking on theatrical waters. Freedom and the theatre are incompatible. For the theatre is a despot, a tyrant to whom you must be willing to pay tribute with every breathing moment of your life. As for earnings, the novitiate is long, the fasting painful and at the end most fortunes in the theatre come from by-products of your art, infrequently from acting itself.

Therefore: know yourself and your desires truly. Granted there are notable exceptions to all formulas, it cannot harm you to take stock of your equipment before casting off on your voyage.

Talent you must have. That indescribable power to create the illusion that you are someone else. And you must know with assurance that you CAN create an illusion. Beauty, or in its absence, personality; strength of body or its compensation in flexibility and expressiveness; and a voice which is not a monotone but which can be developed and whipped into submission; these are essentials. To these fundamentals add determination. Not stubborn, irritating determination, but a long-range determination that has no possible recognition of defeat, one that ploughs through, around or across every obstacle in its path.

Health is needed. A strong body, a rested body, one that can endure day after day of whirling, rushing activity; one that can withstand hours of static waiting, patient immobility.

The desire to be one of a group and the stimulation of gregarious accomplishment are natural beneficial herd instincts. Those instincts should not be denied. They are the basis for normal response and reactions between players, for the fluidity of harmonious scenes, for the team-work of long established companies. The ability to work as one of a group is an estimable quality.

But the courage to close the door, to work alone, away from the bolstering companionship and warmth of Group activity is the test of an artist. In the innermost sanctum you must face yourself and learn, by that communion, the truth and depth of your ambitions. Look into your spiritual and emotional background, into your mental storehouse. Have you consciousness of the spiritual as opposed to the material? Have you sympathy, understanding, patience? Do you respond to the excitement of crises with restrained control? Do you think vaguely, blurring your thought processes with muddled emotion and undisciplined prejudice? Or are your thoughts clear? Translucent? Do they progress logically, crystallizing as they unfold into an edifice unclouded by irrationalisms?

Think clearly, feel deeply and know the strength of spiritual understanding.

Bring to the theatre an education which is as broad as your opportunities. The more you know the more you understand, and the more you understand the clearer is your recognition of the viewpoints of other men and women, and the easier will be your task of interpreting their characters. Read, study, enlarge the horizon of your thought. "Get wisdom, get understanding, forget it not."

Develop the tools of your craft, namely, your voice, your body. Guard both well and train them to instantaneous response.

Make use of sports, of exercises, of dances, but be their master always. They must not master you. Play tennis, learn the freedom of movement, the quickness of eye that tennis gives. Play baseball, learn to jump, to run, to hurl a fast one, but don't, I beg of you, walk like an athlete, shake hands like an athlete or stand like an athlete, unless you are playing the part of an athlete. Learn to dance. Have control of your muscles, whether you dance adagio or swing, but don't swing when you should walk, or waltz when you should run.

Exercise your whole body. Not to create arm-swellings and chest expansions, which in an athlete gain the plaudits of the crowd, but to teach your muscles quick, effortless response, so that when you sit down, stand up, walk, run, move about, turn, twist, or hold yourself in a suspended movement, your audience will be totally unconscious of the mechanics of control.

Remember, from the tip of your toes to the top of your head, there are muscles to be trained like soldiers in an army, ready to be called upon for service to move your body as the body of each portrayed character should be moved: slow or fast, awkward or graceful, crippled or upright, aged or youthful.

Learn to speak, to cry, to whisper, to shout. Walk and breathe, run and laugh. Wake your body and voice into activity and learn through "doing" not "theorizing." Master speech, its rhythm, modulation, volume, dialect. Learn the mumble of illiterates, the stilted artificiality of middle-class snobbery, the gentle, the raucous, the sonorous, the whining. Study, strive, and learn, remembering that only "fools despise wisdom," therefore to be no fool "take fast hold of instruction; let her not go."

Bring as your offering your spirit, thought, body, voice, imagination, truthfulness, enthusiasm, sensitivity. In short: mirror the world and the stars in your understanding and never cease striving for perfection. And when your offerings are heaped high in your arms then in confidence, bring them to the door and knock—knowing at last that you have earned the right to begin.

Reflections from Tony Award Winners

What remains most vivid for me as I reflect upon my two Tony experiences, is the memory of the intense embracing support of the community. And how excited and proud I felt to be a party of this *celebration* of our community.

I try to think of these awards not only as a reminder of a standard of excellence, but as inspiration to challenge myself to take new risks and pursue them with courage and integrity.

Donna Murphy
Tony Award, Actress (Musical), *Passion*, 1994
Tony Award, Actress (Musical), *The King and I*, 1996

I really only remember spurts of the evening of my first Tony Award: putting on my dress during the two commercial breaks and rushing to my seat panicked because I couldn't find my lucky origami star. I wasn't hungry and hadn't eaten in about a week. So when I was finally standing at the podium after what seemed like an endless "I-hope-I-don't-trip" walk to the stage, I had just two thoughts: "What am I going to say?" and "I really want a quarter pounder with cheese!"

Audra McDonald
Tony Award, Featured Actress (Musical), *Carousel*, 1994
Tony Award, Featured Actress (Play), *Master Class*, 1996
Tony Award, Featured Actress (Musical), *Ragtime*, 1998

For many, many years, I felt as if I were happily playing to the orchestra section. Winning the Tony was like looking up and realizing I was, in fact, performing in a three-tiered theater filled with a loving and approving audience. I was physically and emotionally overwhelmed by the honor. I can honestly deem the day I won the Tony as a perfect day in my life. With the recognition, of course, comes an added level of responsibility and pressure. There's no turning back to those "orchestra-only" performances. From then on, the house is always packed with eager and expectant patrons. And I want, with all my heart, for all of them to love what they see.

Faith Prince
Tony Award, Actress (Musical), *Guys and Dolls,* 1992

There was only one thing I ever *intended* to do in my life—and that was to act. Not that I didn't intend to do other important things like make a living or fall in love or take care of my mother when she needed me, or any other missions born of necessity or need or simply the instinct to survive—but to act was a *choice,* and in my case a *choice for life* (It's one of those unexplainable things some people do that has no particular historic reason nor discernible antecedent). Simply a choice—a *beginning!* And every effort to follow a *deposit* into that great black box—*expectation.*

"Why do I do this? Why does anyone do this?" I'd ask this question at every juncture or introspective pause for the next twenty years. And one day it all came abundantly clear to me—a Tony! Now, if you can imagine what it would be like to feel, in an instant, an all encompassing affection, good will, and an overwhelming acceptance of your work by an entire community of what was to me a *choice for life.* Then, you will just begin to get an inkling of what it meant to me to receive an acknowledgment of this kind. Life can no longer have the same purpose; loving can no longer bear resemblance to any other experience or event even previously anticipated.

Judd Hirsch
Tony Award, Actor (Play), *I'm Not Rappaport,* 1986
Tony Award, Actor (Play), *Conversations With My Father,* 1992

Receiving my first Tony was a night I will always cherish. I have a great passion for theatre and I have always wanted to be a choreographer. The fact that I have been recognized by my peers is a dream realized. I'm living proof that imagination and preparation can beget the biggest dreams for the shortest girl from the smallest town.

Susan Stroman
Tony Award, Choreographer, *Crazy for You,* 1992
Tony Award, Choreographer, *Show Boat,* 1995
Tony Award, Choreographer, *Contact,* 2000

I had suddenly been awarded "Best Director" by all those who best know. I was ecstatic. I walked very lightly, supported by that thought, but I carried the heavy load of all those who had made it possible. Would I now, in this moment, be able to as "Best" give them their proper due. That, magic moment of serenity, came and swiftly passed. It was Theatre and like all good theatre impossible to describe. You had to be there.

Lloyd Richards
Tony Award, Director (Play), *Fences*, 1987

Every time I start a project, I hope that my work will impact upon an audience in some meaningful way—that a connection will be made. To the extent that the Tony Award suggests that I have succeeded in touching my peers and colleagues—those who understand what goes into a production to make that connection happen—the Tony Award is the most gratifying symbol of success to me.

Jerry Zaks
Tony Award, Director (Play), *The House of Blue Leaves*, 1986
Tony Award, Director (Play), *Lend Me a Tenor*, 1989
Tony Award, Director (Play), *Six Degrees of Separation*, 1991
Tony Award, Director (Musical), *Guys and Dolls*, 1992

The most exciting part about receiving the Tony is when, after the nominees are read, you hear, "And the winner is . . ." Once your name is spoken your heart jumps into your throat. You rise, afraid you've misheard what was said—somehow you weave your way down the aisle, shakily negotiating the stairs, find your way across the stage to the presenter, the Tony gets plunked in your hands—and then the terror begins. You want to thank everyone that's touched the production for which you are winning. It's everybody *else* that has made you look good that deserves the award, but somehow it's *you* receiving it. How can you thank them all publicly? How can you get off the stage immediately and stop slowing down the show with unmitigated gratitude? If anyone has the answer, let me know. And may you all win Tonys!

Tommy Tune
Tony Award, Featured Actor (Musical), *Seesaw*, 1974
Tony Award, Choreographer, *A Day in Hollywood/*
A Night in the Ukraine, 1980
Tony Award, Director (Musical), *Nine*, 1982
Tony Award, Actor (Musical), *My One and Only*, 1983
Tony Award, Choreographer, *My One and Only*, 1983
Tony Award, Director (Musical), *Grand Hotel, The Musical*, 1990
Tony Award, Director (Musical), *The Will Rogers Follies*, 1991
Tony Award, Choreographer, *The Will Rogers Follies*, 1991

The Tony Award is something I have spent half my life dreaming of achieving and striving to be worthy of. Now, upon reflection, I know no one person wins a Tony. A team of collaborative artists gives birth to an idea and carries it with devotion through its childhood and into its adulthood.

To me, the Tony is my director calling at midnight with a new idea, it's my wonderful actors figuring out how to use a costume to best advantage, or it's my cherished drapers taking me aside to look at a new way to put two trims together for a better effect on a costume.

My Tony belongs more to these loving and brilliantly talented people than to me. I am so lucky to have them!

Ann Hould-Ward
Tony Award, Costume Designer, *Beauty and the Beast*, 1994

Having now had 13 Tony strikeouts in 16 times at bat, I'm comfortable with losing out by now. But on the last occasion I won the Tony Award, it was surprisingly heart-warming to suddenly realize that all the remarkable craftspeople who had contributed so gloriously to the finished settings could feel terrific knowing that their labors had been acknowledged by the Theatre Community. And, coming—as I do—from a background that encouraged the belief: "it's not a matter of win or lose, but how you play the game," it felt great, nonetheless, not to have to go through the rest of the evening sporting a graceful grin, but to let loose instead with a big, silly smile.

Tony Walton
Tony Award, Scenic Designer, *Pippin*, 1973
Tony Award, Scenic Designer, *The House of Blue Leaves*, 1986
Tony Award, Scenic Designer, *Guys and Dolls*, 1992

The 1940s

"**I**n 1948, the second year that the Tony Awards were presented, I had a non-speaking part in Robinson Jeffers' 'Medea,' and Judith Anderson won a Tony for her brilliant performance. It was the first play I had been in on Broadway. I do not remember dreaming of such an award.

Nineteen years later I received a nomination for my performance as Julia in Edward Albee's 'A Delicate Balance' (and won), and later received nominations for a leading performance in Oliver Hailey's 'Father's Day' and for a featured performance in 'Deathtrap' (and did not win) .

Looking back, it was the nomination that meant the most to me every time. I admired the actresses in my categories and was proud to be listed with them.

The thrill of winning lasts a minute. The memory of rehearsing, playing the parts, sharing them with audiences lasts much longer. And in some special way the recognition of the Tony committee makes the memories seem even dearer.

Each time I felt that the part won—the playwright won—and I accepted the Award and the scroll for them. So I treasure both and always will."

Marian Seldes
Featured Actress (Play), *A Delicate Balance*

1947

ACTORS (PLAY)
☆ José Ferrer, *Cyrano de Bergerac*
☆ Fredric March, *Years Ago*

ACTRESSES (PLAY)
☆ Ingrid Bergman, *Joan of Lorraine*
☆ Helen Hayes, *Happy Birthday*

FEATURED ACTRESS (PLAY)
☆ Patricia Neal, *Another Part of the Forest*

FEATURED ACTOR (MUSICAL)
☆ David Wayne, *Finian's Rainbow*

PLAYWRIGHT
☆ Arthur Miller, *All My Sons*

DIRECTOR
☆ Elia Kazan, *All My Sons*

COSTUMES
☆ Lucinda Ballard, *Happy Birthday* / *Another Part of the Forest* /
  Street Scene / *John Loves Mary* / *The Chocolate Soldier*

SCENIC DESIGNER
☆ David Ffolkes, *Henry VIII*

CHOREOGRAPHERS
☆ Agnes de Mille, *Brigadoon*
☆ Michael Kidd, *Finian's Rainbow*

SCORE
☆ Kurt Weill, *Street Scene*

SPECIAL AWARDS
☆ Dora Chamberlain, for unfailing courtesy as treasurer of the
  Martin Beck Theatre.
☆ Mr. and Mrs. Ira Katzenberg, for enthusiasm as inveterate
  first-nighters.
☆ Jules Leventhal, for the season's most prolific backer and
  producer.
☆ Burns Mantle, for the annual publication of *The Ten Best Plays*.
☆ P. A. MacDonald, for intricate construction for the production
  If the Shoe Fits.
☆ Vincent Sardi, Sr., for providing a transient home and com-
  fort station for theatre folk at Sardi's for 20 years.

1948

PLAY
☆ *Mister Roberts* by Thomas Heggen and Joshua Logan based on the Thomas Heggen novel

LEADING ACTORS (PLAY)
☆ Henry Fonda, *Mister Roberts*
☆ Paul Kelly, *Command Decision*
☆ Basil Rathbone, *The Heiress*

LEADING ACTRESSES (PLAY)
☆ Judith Anderson, *Medea*
☆ Katharine Cornell, *Antony and Cleopatra*
☆ Jessica Tandy, *A Streetcar Named Desire*

LEADING ACTOR (MUSICAL)
☆ Paul Hartman, *Angel in the Wings*

LEADING ACTRESS (MUSICAL)
☆ Grace Hartman, *Angel in the Wings*

PRODUCER
☆ Leland Hayward, *Mister Roberts*

AUTHORS
☆ Thomas Heggen and Joshua Logan, *Mister Roberts*

DIRECTOR
☆ Joshua Logan, *Mister Roberts*

SCENIC DESIGNER
☆ Horace Armistead, *The Medium*

COSTUMES
☆ Mary Percy Schenck, *The Heiress*

CHOREOGRAPHER
☆ Jerome Robbins, *High Button Shoes*

STAGE TECHNICIAN
☆ George Gebhardt

CONDUCTOR AND MUSICAL DIRECTOR
☆ Max Meth, *Finian's Rainbow*

SPECIAL AWARDS
☆ June Lockhart, *For Love or Money*, for outstanding performance by a newcomer.
☆ James Whitmore, *Command Decision*, for outstanding performance by a newcomer.

☆ Cast of T*he Importance of Being Earnest*, directed by John Gielgud, for outstanding foreign company.

☆ Mary Martin, A*nnie Get Your Gun*, for out of town performance.

☆ Joe E. Brown, H*arvey*, for out of town performance.

☆ Experimental Theatre, Inc., John Garfield accepting.

☆ Robert W. Dowling, president of City Investing Company, owner of several theatres in New York.

☆ Paul Beisman, operator of the American Theatre, St. Louis.

☆ Rosamond Gilder, editor, T*heatre Arts*, for contribution to theatre through a publication.

☆ Robert Porterfield, Virginia Barter Theatre, for contribution to the development of regional theatre.

☆ Vera Allen, for distinguished Wing volunteer during the War and after.

☆ George Pierce, for twenty-five years of courteous and efficient service as a backstage doorman (Empire Theatre).

1949

MUSICAL

☆ *Kiss Me, Kate*. Music and lyrics by Cole Porter, book by Bella and Samuel Spewack. Produced by Saint-Subber and Lemuel Ayers.

PLAY

☆ *Death of a Salesman* by Arthur Miller. Produced by Kermit Bloomgarden and Walter Fried.

LEADING ACTOR (PLAY)

☆ Rex Harrison, A*nne of the Thousand Days*

LEADING ACTRESS (PLAY)

☆ Martita Hunt, T*he Madwoman of Chaillot*

FEATURED ACTOR (PLAY)

☆ Arthur Kennedy, *Death of a Salesman*

FEATURED ACTRESS (PLAY)

☆ Shirley Booth, *Goodbye, My Fancy*

LEADING ACTOR (MUSICAL)

☆ Ray Bolger, W*here's Charley?*

LEADING ACTRESS (MUSICAL)

☆ Nanette Fabray, *Love Life*

PRODUCERS (PLAY)
☆ Kermit Bloomgarden and Walter Fried, *Death of a Salesman*

AUTHOR (PLAY)
☆ Arthur Miller, *Death of a Salesman*

DIRECTOR
☆ Elia Kazan, *Death of a Salesman*

PRODUCERS (MUSICAL)
☆ Saint-Subber and Lemuel Ayers, *Kiss Me, Kate*

AUTHORS (MUSICAL)
☆ Bella and Samuel Spewack, *Kiss Me, Kate*

COMPOSER AND LYRICIST
☆ Cole Porter, *Kiss Me, Kate*

COSTUMES
☆ Lemuel Ayers, *Kiss Me, Kate*

SCENIC DESIGNER
☆ Jo Mielziner, *Sleepy Hollow / Summer and Smoke / Anne of the Thousand Days / Death of a Salesman / South Pacific*

CHOREOGRAPHER
☆ Gower Champion, *Lend an Ear*

CONDUCTOR AND MUSICAL DIRECTOR
☆ Max Meth, *As the Girls Go*

The 1950s

"There are two types of people. One type asserts that awards mean nothing to them. The second type breaks out into tears upon receiving an award, and thanks their mother, father, children, the producer, the director—and, if they can crowd it in—the American Baseball League.

However, I believe that people in the theatre who receive this award have a special feeling that makes them cherish the winning of a Tony. It prevents them from going on effusively. The Tony has a special value. It was created to award distinguished achievement in the theatre."

Dore Schary
Author (Play), *Sunrise at Campobello*

HAROLD PRINCE, RICHARD RODGERS, AND ETHEL MERMAN

1950

MUSICAL
☆ *South Pacific.* Music by Richard Rodgers, lyrics by Oscar Hammerstein II, book by Oscar Hammerstein II and Joshua Logan. Produced by Leland Hayward, Oscar Hammerstein II, Joshua Logan, and Richard Rodgers.

PLAY
☆ *The Cocktail Party* by T.S. Eliot. Produced by Gilbert Miller.

LEADING ACTOR (PLAY)
☆ Sidney Blackmer, *Come Back, Little Sheba*

LEADING ACTRESS (PLAY)
☆ Shirley Booth, *Come Back, Little Sheba*

LEADING ACTOR (MUSICAL)
☆ Ezio Pinza, *South Pacific*

LEADING ACTRESS (MUSICAL)
☆ Mary Martin, *South Pacific*

FEATURED ACTOR (MUSICAL)
☆ Myron McCormick, *South Pacific*

FEATURED ACTRESS (MUSICAL)
☆ Juanita Hall, *South Pacific*

AUTHOR (PLAY)
☆ T.S. Eliot, *The Cocktail Party*

PRODUCER (PLAY)
☆ Gilbert Miller, *The Cocktail Party*

DIRECTOR
☆ Joshua Logan, *South Pacific*

AUTHORS (MUSICAL)
☆ Oscar Hammerstein II and Joshua Logan, *South Pacific*

PRODUCERS (MUSICAL)
☆ Richard Rodgers, Oscar Hammerstein II, Leland Hayward, and Joshua Logan, *South Pacific*

COMPOSER
☆ Richard Rodgers, *South Pacific*

SCENIC DESIGNER
☆ Jo Mielziner, *The Innocents*

COSTUME DESIGNER
☆ Aline Bernstein, *Regina*

CHOREOGRAPHER
☆ Helen Tamiris, *Touch and Go*

CONDUCTOR AND MUSICAL DIRECTOR
☆ Maurice Abravanel, *Regina*

STAGE TECHNICIAN
☆ Joe Lynn, master propertyman, *Miss Liberty*

SPECIAL AWARDS
☆ Maurice Evans, for work he did in guiding the City Center Theatre Company through a highly successful season.
☆ Philip Faversham, volunteer worker for the American Theatre Wing's hospital program.
☆ Brock Pemberton (posthumous), original chairman of the Tony Awards.

1951

MUSICAL
☆ *Guys and Dolls*. Music and lyrics by Frank Loesser, book by Jo Swerling and Abe Burrows. Produced by Cy Feuer and Ernest H. Martin.

PLAY
☆ *The Rose Tattoo* by Tennessee Williams. Produced by Cheryl Crawford.

LEADING ACTOR (PLAY)
☆ Claude Rains, *Darkness at Noon*

LEADING ACTRESS (PLAY)
☆ Uta Hagen, *The Country Girl*

FEATURED ACTOR (PLAY)
☆ Eli Wallach, *The Rose Tattoo*

FEATURED ACTRESS (PLAY)
☆ Maureen Stapleton, *The Rose Tattoo*

LEADING ACTOR (MUSICAL)
☆ Robert Alda, *Guys and Dolls*

LEADING ACTRESS (MUSICAL)
☆ Ethel Merman, *Call Me Madam*

FEATURED ACTOR (MUSICAL)
☆ Russell Nype, *Call Me Madam*

FEATURED ACTRESS (MUSICAL)
☆ Isabel Bigley, *Guys and Dolls*

AUTHOR (PLAY)
☆ Tennessee Williams, *The Rose Tattoo*

PRODUCER (PLAY)
☆ Cheryl Crawford, *The Rose Tattoo*

DIRECTOR
☆ George S. Kaufman, *Guys and Dolls*

AUTHOR (MUSICAL)
☆ Jo Swerling and Abe Burrows, *Guys and Dolls*

PRODUCER (MUSICAL)
☆ Cy Feuer and Ernest H. Martin, *Guys and Dolls*

MUSICAL SCORE
☆ Irving Berlin, *Call Me Madam*

COMPOSER AND LYRICIST
☆ Frank Loesser, *Guys and Dolls*

SCENIC DESIGNER
☆ Boris Aronson, *The Rose Tattoo* / *The Country Girl* / *Season in the Sun*

COSTUME DESIGNER
☆ Miles White, *Bless You All*

CHOREOGRAPHER
☆ Michael Kidd, *Guys and Dolls*

CONDUCTOR AND MUSICAL DIRECTOR
☆ Lehman Engel, *The Consul*

STAGE TECHNICIAN
☆ Richard Raven, master electrician, *The Autumn Garden*

SPECIAL AWARD
☆ Ruth Green, for her services as a volunteer in arranging reservations and seating for the five Tony Award events (1947–1951).

1952

MUSICAL
☆ The *King and* I. Music by Richard Rodgers, book and lyrics by Oscar Hammerstein II.

PLAY
☆ The *Fourposter* by Jan de Hartog.

LEADING ACTOR (PLAY)
☆ José Ferrer, The *Shrike*

LEADING ACTRESS (PLAY)
☆ Julie Harris, I *Am a Camera*

FEATURED ACTOR (PLAY)
☆ John Cromwell, *Point of No Return*

FEATURED ACTRESS (PLAY)
☆ Marian Winters, I *Am a Camera*

LEADING ACTOR (MUSICAL)
☆ Phil Silvers, *Top Banana*

LEADING ACTRESS (MUSICAL)
☆ Gertrude Lawrence, The *King and* I

FEATURED ACTOR (MUSICAL)
☆ Yul Brynner, The *King and* I

FEATURED ACTRESS (MUSICAL)
☆ Helen Gallagher, *Pal Joey*

DIRECTOR
☆ José Ferrer, The *Shrike* / The *Fourposter* / *Stalag* 17

SCENIC DESIGNER
☆ Jo Mielziner, The *King and* I

COSTUME DESIGNER
☆ Irene Sharaff, The *King and* I

CHOREOGRAPHER
☆ Robert Alton, *Pal Joey*

CONDUCTOR AND MUSICAL DIRECTOR
☆ Max Meth, *Pal Joey*

STAGE TECHNICIAN
☆ Peter Feller, master carpenter, *Call Me Madam*

SPECIAL AWARDS

☆ Judy Garland, for an important contribution to the revival of vaudeville through her recent stint at the Palace Theatre.

☆ Edward Kook, for contributing to and encouraging the development of stage lighting and electronics.

☆ Charles Boyer, for distinguished performance in *Don Juan in Hell*, thereby assisting in a new theatre trend.

1953

MUSICAL

☆ *Wonderful Town*. Music by Leonard Bernstein, lyrics by Betty Comden and Adolph Green, book by Joseph Fields and Jerome Chodorov. Produced by Robert Fryer.

PLAY

☆ *The Crucible* by Arthur Miller. Produced by Kermit Bloomgarden.

LEADING ACTOR (PLAY)

☆ Tom Ewell, *The Seven Year Itch*

LEADING ACTRESS (PLAY)

☆ Shirley Booth, *The Time of the Cuckoo*

FEATURED ACTOR (PLAY)

☆ John Williams, *Dial M for Murder*

FEATURED ACTRESS (PLAY)

☆ Beatrice Straight, *The Crucible*

LEADING ACTOR (MUSICAL)

☆ Thomas Mitchell, *Hazel Flagg*

LEADING ACTRESS (MUSICAL)

☆ Rosalind Russell, *Wonderful Town*

FEATURED ACTOR (MUSICAL)

☆ Hiram Sherman, *Two's Company*

FEATURED ACTRESS (MUSICAL)

☆ Sheila Bond, *Wish You Were Here*

AUTHOR (PLAY)

☆ Arthur Miller, *The Crucible*

PRODUCER (PLAY)

☆ Kermit Bloomgarden, *The Crucible*

DIRECTOR
☆ Joshua Logan, *Picnic*

AUTHORS (MUSICAL)
☆ Joseph Fields and Jerome Chodorov, *Wonderful Town*

PRODUCER (MUSICAL)
☆ Robert Fryer, *Wonderful Town*

COMPOSER
☆ Leonard Bernstein, *Wonderful Town*

SCENIC DESIGNER
☆ Raoul Pène du Bois, *Wonderful Town*

COSTUME DESIGNER
☆ Miles White, *Hazel Flagg*

CHOREOGRAPHER
☆ Donald Saddler, *Wonderful Town*

CONDUCTOR AND MUSICAL DIRECTOR
☆ Lehman Engel, *Wonderful Town* and Gilbert and Sullivan Season

STAGE TECHNICIAN
☆ Abe Kurnit, *Wish You Were Here*

SPECIAL AWARDS
☆ Beatrice Lillie, for *An Evening with Beatrice Lillie.*
☆ Danny Kaye, for heading a variety bill at the Palace Theatre.
☆ Equity Community Theatre

1954

MUSICAL
☆ *Kismet.* Music by Alexander Borodin, adapted and with lyrics by Robert Wright and George Forrest, book by Charles Lederer and Luther Davis. Produced by Charles Lederer.

PLAY
☆ *The Teahouse of the August Moon* by John Patrick. Produced by Maurice Evans and George Schaefer.

LEADING ACTOR (PLAY)
☆ David Wayne, *The Teahouse of the August Moon*

LEADING ACTRESS (PLAY)
☆ Audrey Hepburn, *Ondine*

FEATURED ACTOR (PLAY)
☆ John Kerr, *Tea and Sympathy*

FEATURED ACTRESS (PLAY)
☆ Jo Van Fleet, *The Trip to Bountiful*

LEADING ACTOR (MUSICAL)
☆ Alfred Drake, *Kismet*

LEADING ACTRESS (MUSICAL)
☆ Dolores Gray, *Carnival in Flanders*

FEATURED ACTOR (MUSICAL)
☆ Harry Belafonte, *John Murray Anderson's Almanac*

FEATURED ACTRESS (MUSICAL)
☆ Gwen Verdon, *Can-Can*

AUTHOR (PLAY)
☆ John Patrick, *The Teahouse of the August Moon*

PRODUCER (PLAY)
☆ Maurice Evans and George Schaefer, *The Teahouse of the August Moon*

DIRECTOR
☆ Alfred Lunt, *Ondine*

AUTHOR (MUSICAL)
☆ Charles Lederer and Luther Davis, *Kismet*

PRODUCER (MUSICAL)
☆ Charles Lederer, *Kismet*

COMPOSER
☆ Alexander Borodin, *Kismet*

SCENIC DESIGNER
☆ Peter Larken, *Ondine* and *The Teahouse of the August Moon*

COSTUME DESIGNER
☆ Richard Whorf, *Ondine*

CHOREOGRAPHER
☆ Michael Kidd, *Can-Can*

MUSICAL CONDUCTOR
☆ Louis Adrian, *Kismet*

STAGE TECHNICIAN
☆ John Davis, *Picnic*, for constant good work as a theatre electrician.

1955

MUSICAL
☆ *The Pajama Game*. Music and lyrics by Richard Adler and Jerry Ross, book by George Abbott and Richard Bissell, Produced by Frederick Brisson, Robert Griffith, and Harold S. Prince.

PLAY
☆ *The Desperate Hours* by Joseph Hayes. Produced by Howard Erskine and Joseph Hayes.

LEADING ACTOR (PLAY)
☆ Alfred Lunt, *Quadrille*

LEADING ACTRESS (PLAY)
☆ Nancy Kelly, *The Bad Seed*

FEATURED ACTOR (PLAY)
☆ Francis L. Sullivan, *Witness for the Prosecution*

FEATURED ACTRESS (PLAY)
☆ Patricia Jessel, *Witness for the Prosecution*

LEADING ACTOR (MUSICAL)
☆ Walter Slezak, *Fanny*

LEADING ACTRESS (MUSICAL)
☆ Mary Martin, *Peter Pan*

FEATURED ACTOR (MUSICAL)
☆ Cyril Ritchard, *Peter Pan*

FEATURED ACTRESS (MUSICAL)
☆ Carol Haney, *The Pajama Game*

AUTHOR (PLAY)
☆ Joseph Hayes, *The Desperate Hours*

PRODUCER (PLAY)
☆ Howard Erskine and Joseph Hayes, *The Desperate Hours*

DIRECTOR
☆ Robert Montgomery, *The Desperate Hours*

Photo: Anita and Steve Shevett

GEORGE ABBOTT

Authors (Musical)
☆ George Abbott and Richard Bissell, The Pajama Game

Producers (Musical)
☆ Frederick Brisson, Robert Griffith and Harold S. Prince, The
    Pajama Game

Composer and Lyricist
☆ Richard Adler and Jerry Ross, The Pajama Game

Scenic Designer
☆ Oliver Messel, House of Flowers

Costume Designer
☆ Cecil Beaton, Quadrille

CHOREOGRAPHER
☆ Bob Fosse, The Pajama Game

CONDUCTOR AND MUSICAL DIRECTOR
☆ Thomas Schippers, The Saint of Bleecker Street

STAGE TECHNICIAN
☆ Richard Rodda, Peter Pan

SPECIAL AWARDS
☆ Proscenium Productions, an Off-Broadway company at the Cherry Lane Theatre, for generally high quality and viewpoint shown in The Way of the World and Thieves Carnival.

1956

MUSICAL
☆ Damn Yankees. Music and lyrics by Richard Adler and Jerry Ross, book by George Abbott and Douglass Wallop. Produced by Frederick Brisson, Robert Griffith, and Harold S. Prince in association with Albert B. Taylor.
Pipe Dream. Music by Richard Rodgers, book and lyrics by Oscar Hammerstein II. Produced by Rodgers and Hammerstein.

PLAY
Bus Stop by William Inge. Produced by Robert Whitehead and Roger L. Stevens.
Cat on a Hot Tin Roof by Tennessee Williams. Produced by The Playwrights' Company.
☆ The Diary of Anne Frank by Frances Goodrich and Albert Hackett. Produced by Kermit Bloomgarden.
Tiger at the Gates by Jean Giraudoux, adapted by Christopher Fry. Produced by Robert L. Joseph, The Playwrights' Company and Henry M. Margolis.
The Chalk Garden by Enid Bagnold. Produced by Irene Mayer Selznick.

LEADING ACTOR (PLAY)
Ben Gazzara, A Hatful of Rain
Boris Karloff, The Lark
☆ Paul Muni, Inherit the Wind
Michael Redgrave, Tiger at the Gates
Edward G. Robinson, Middle of the Night

Leading Actress (Play)

Barbara Bel Geddes, *Cat on a Hot Tin Roof*
Gladys Cooper, *The Chalk Garden*
Ruth Gordon, *The Matchmaker*
☆   Julie Harris, *The Lark*
Siobhan McKenna, *The Chalk Garden*
Susan Strasberg, *The Diary of Anne Frank*

Featured Actor (Play)

☆   Ed Begley, *Inherit the Wind*
Anthony Franciosa, *A Hatful of Rain*
Andy Griffith, *No Time for Sergeants*
Anthony Quayle, *Tamburlaine the Great*
Fritz Weaver, *The Chalk Garden*

Featured Actress (Play)

Diane Cilento, *Tiger at the Gates*
Anne Jackson, *Middle of the Night*
☆   Una Merkel, *The Ponder Heart*
Elaine Stritch, *Bus Stop*

Leading Actor (Musical)

Stephen Douglass, *Damn Yankees*
William Johnson, *Pipe Dream*
☆   Ray Walston, *Damn Yankees*

Leading Actress (Musical)

Carol Channing, *The Vamp*
☆   Gwen Verdon, *Damn Yankees*
Nancy Walker, *Phoenix '55*

Featured Actor (Musical)

☆   Russ Brown, *Damn Yankees*
Mike Kellin, *Pipe Dream*
Will Mahoney, City Center *Finian's Rainbow*
Scott Merrill, *The Threepenny Opera*

Featured Actress (Musical)

Rae Allen, *Damn Yankees*
Pat Carroll, *Catch a Star*
☆   Lotte Lenya, *The Threepenny Opera*
Judy Tyler, *Pipe Dream*

Authors (Play)

☆   Frances Goodrich and Albert Hackett, *The Diary of Anne Frank*

PRODUCER (PLAY)

☆   Kermit Bloomgarden, *The Diary of Anne Frank*

DIRECTOR (PLAY)

Joseph Anthony, *The Lark*
Harold Clurman, *Bus Stop* / *Pipe Dream* / *Tiger at the Gates*
☆   Tyrone Guthrie, ☆ *The Matchmaker* / *Six Characters in Search of an Author* / *Tamburlaine the Great*
Garson Kanin, *The Diary of Anne Frank*
Elia Kazan, *Cat on a Hot Tin Roof*
Albert Marre, *The Chalk Garden*
Herman Shumlin, *Inherit the Wind*

AUTHORS (MUSICAL)

☆   George Abbott and Douglass Wallop, *Damn Yankees*

PRODUCERS (MUSICAL)

☆   Frederick Brisson, Robert Griffith and Harold S. Prince in association with Albert B. Taylor, *Damn Yankees*

COMPOSER AND LYRICIST

☆   Richard Adler and Jerry Ross, *Damn Yankees*

SCENIC DESIGNER

Boris Aronson, *The Diary of Anne Frank* / *Bus Stop* / *Once Upon a Tailor* / *A View from the Bridge*
Ben Edwards, *The Ponder Heart* / *Someone Waiting* / *The Honeys*
☆   Peter Larkin, *Inherit the Wind* / *No Time for Sergeants*
Jo Mielziner, *Cat on a Hot Tin Roof* / *The Lark* / *Middle of the Night* / *Pipe Dream*
Raymond Sovey, *The Great Sebastians*

COSTUME DESIGNER

Mainbocher, *The Great Sebastians*
☆   Alvin Colt, *The Lark* / *Phoenix '55* / ☆ *Pipe Dream*
Helene Pons, *The Diary of Anne Frank* / *Heavenly Twins* / *A View from the Bridge*

CHOREOGRAPHER

Robert Alton, *The Vamp*
☆   Bob Fosse, *Damn Yankees*
Boris Runanin, *Phoenix '55* / *Pipe Dream*
Anna Sokolow, *Red Roses for Me*

STAGE TECHNICIAN

Larry Bland, carpenter, *Middle of the Night* / *The Ponder Heart* / *Porgy and Bess*
☆   Harry Green, electrician and sound man, *Middle of the Night* / *Damn Yankees*

Photo: Anita and Steve Shevett

BOB FOSSE AND GWEN VERDON

SPECIAL AWARDS

☆ City Center
☆ Fourth Street Chekhov Theatre
☆ The Shakespearewrights
☆ The *Threepenny Opera*, distinguished Off-Broadway production. Produced by Carmen Capalbo and Stanley Chase.
☆ The Theatre Collection of the N.Y. Public Library on its twenty-fifth anniversary, for its distinguished service to the theatre.

1957

MUSICAL

Bells Are Ringing. Music by Jule Styne, book and lyrics by Betty Comden and Adolph Green. Produced by The Theatre Guild.

Candide. Music by Leonard Bernstein, lyrics by Richard Wilbur, book by Lillian Hellman. Produced by Ethel Linder Reiner in association with Lester Osterman, Jr.

☆ *My Fair Lady*. Music by Frederick Loewe, book and lyrics by Alan Jay Lerner. Produced by Herman Levin.

The Most Happy Fella. Music, lyrics, and book by Frank Loesser. Produced by Kermit Bloomgarden and Lynn Loesser.

PLAY

☆ *Long Day's Journey Into Night* by Eugene O'Neill. Produced by Leigh Connell, Theodore Mann, and José Quintero.

Separate Tables by Terence Rattigan. Produced by The Producers Theatre and Hecht-Lancaster.

The Potting Shed by Graham Greene. Produced by Carmen Capalbo and Stanley Chase.

The Waltz of the Toreadors by Jean Anouilh, Translated by Lucienne Hill. Produced by The Producers Theatre (Robert Whitehead).

LEADING ACTOR (PLAY)

Maurice Evans, *The Apple Cart*
Wilfred Hyde-White, *The Reluctant Debutante*
☆ Fredric March, *Long Day's Journey Into Night*
Eric Portman, *Separate Tables*
Ralph Richardson, *The Waltz of the Toreadors*
Cyril Ritchard, *A Visit to a Small Planet*

LEADING ACTRESS (PLAY)

Florence Eldridge, *Long Day's Journey Into Night*
☆ Margaret Leighton, *Separate Tables*
Rosalind Russell, *Auntie Mame*
Sybil Thorndike, *The Potting Shed*

FEATURED ACTOR (PLAY)

☆ Frank Conroy, *The Potting Shed*
Eddie Mayehoff, *A Visit to a Small Planet*
William Podmore, *Separate Tables*
Jason Robards, Jr., *Long Day's Journey Into Night*

FEATURED ACTRESS (PLAY)

☆ Peggy Cass, *Auntie Mame*
Anna Massey, *The Reluctant Debutante*
Beryl Measor, *Separate Tables*
Mildred Natwick, *The Waltz of the Toreadors*
Phyllis Neilson-Terry, *Separate Tables*

Diana Van Der Vlis, *The Happiest Millionaire*

LEADING ACTOR (MUSICAL)
☆ Rex Harrison, *My Fair Lady*
Fernando Lamas, *Happy Hunting*
Robert Weede, *The Most Happy Fella*

LEADING ACTRESS (MUSICAL)
Julie Andrews, *My Fair Lady*
☆ Judy Holliday, *Bells Are Ringing*
Ethel Merman, *Happy Hunting*

FEATURED ACTOR (MUSICAL)
☆ Sydney Chaplin, *Bells Are Ringing*
Robert Coote, *My Fair Lady*
Stanley Holloway, *My Fair Lady*

FEATURED ACTRESS (MUSICAL)
☆ Edith Adams, *Li'l Abner*
Virginia Gibson, *Happy Hunting*
Irra Petina, *Candide*
Jo Sullivan, *The Most Happy Fella*

AUTHOR (PLAY)
☆ Eugene O'Neill, *Long Day's Journey Into Night*

PRODUCER (PLAY)
☆ Leigh Connell, Theodore Mann and José Quintero, *Long Day's Journey Into Night*

DIRECTOR
Joseph Anthony, *A Clearing in the Woods*
Joseph Anthony, *The Most Happy Fella*
Harold Clurman, *The Waltz of the Toreadors*
Peter Glenville, *Separate Tables*
☆ Moss Hart, *My Fair Lady*
José Quintero, *Long Day's Journey Into Night*

AUTHOR (MUSICAL)
☆ Alan Jay Lerner, *My Fair Lady*

PRODUCER (MUSICAL)
☆ Herman Levin, *My Fair Lady*

COMPOSER
☆ Frederick Loewe, *My Fair Lady*

CONDUCTOR AND MUSICAL DIRECTOR
☆ Franz Allers, *My Fair Lady*

Herbert Greene, *The Most Happy Fella*
Samual Krachmalnick, *Candide*

SCENIC DESIGNER
Boris Aronson, *A Hole in the Head* / *Small War on Murray Hill*
Ben Edwards, *The Waltz of the Toreadors*
George Jenkins, *The Happiest Millionaire* / *Too Late the Phalarope*
Donald Oenslager, *Major Barbara*
☆   Oliver Smith, *A Clearing in the Woods* / *Candide* / *Auntie Mame* /
    ☆ *My Fair Lady* / *Eugenia* / *A Visit to a Small Planet*

COSTUME DESIGNER
☆   Cecil Beaton, *Little Glass Clock* / ☆ *My Fair Lady*
Alvin Colt, *Li'l Abner* / *The Sleeping Prince*
Dorothy Jeakins, *Major Barbara* / *Too Late the Phalarope*
Irene Sharaff, *Candide* / *Happy Hunting* / *Shangri-La* / *Small War on
    Murray Hill*

CHOREOGRAPHER
Hanya Holm, *My Fair Lady*
☆   Michael Kidd, *Li'l Abner*
Dania Krupska, *The Most Happy Fella*
Jerome Robbins and Bob Fosse, *Bells Are Ringing*

STAGE TECHNICIAN
Thomas Fitzgerald, sound man, *Long Day's Journey Into Night*
Joseph Harbach, carpenter, *Auntie Mame*
☆   Howard McDonald, (Posthumous), carpenter, *Major Barbara*

SPECIAL AWARDS
☆   American Shakespeare Festival, Stratford, Connecticut
☆   Jean-Louis Barrault—French Repertory
☆   Robert Russell Bennett
☆   William Hammerstein
☆   Paul Shyre

1958

MUSICAL
West Side Story. Music by Leonard Bernstein, lyrics by Stephen
    Sondheim, book by Arthur Laurents. Produced by Robert
    Griffith and Harold S. Prince.
New Girl in Town. Music and lyrics by Bob Merrill, book by
    George Abbott. Produced by Robert Griffith and Harold
    S. Prince.

☆ T*he Music Man.* Music and lyrics by Meredith Willson, book by Meredith Willson and Franklin Lacey. Produced by Kermit Bloomgarden and Herbert Greene, in association with Frank Productions.

O*h, Captain!* Music and lyrics by Jay Livingston and Ray Evans, book by Al Morgan and José Ferrer. Produced by Howard Merrill and Theatre Corporation of America.

J*amaica.* Music by Harold Arlen, lyrics by E.Y. Harburg, book by E.Y. Harburg and Fred Saidy. Produced by David Merrick.

PLAY

T*he Rope Dancers* by Morton Wishengrad. Produced by The Playwrights Company and Gilbert Miller.

T*wo for the Seesaw* by William Gibson. Produced by Fred Coe.

T*ime Remembered* by Jean Anouilh. English version by Patricia Moyes. Produced by The Playwrights Company, in association with Milton Sperling.

T*he Dark at the Top of the Stairs* by William Inge. Produced by Saint-Subber and Elia Kazan.

L*ook Back in Anger* by John Osborne. Produced by David Merrick.

L*ook Homeward, Angel* by Ketti Frings. Produced by Kermit Bloomgarden and Theatre 200, Inc.

R*omanoff and Juliet* by Peter Ustinov. Produced by David Merrick.

☆ S*unrise at Campobello* by Dore Schary. Produced by Lawrence Langner, Theresa Helburn, Armina Marshall, and Dore Schary.

LEADING ACTOR (PLAY)

☆ Ralph Bellamy, S*unrise at Campobello*
Richard Burton, T*ime Remembered*
Hugh Griffith, L*ook Homeward, Angel*
Laurence Olivier, T*he Entertainer*
Anthony Perkins, L*ook Homeward, Angel*
Peter Ustinov, R*omanoff and Juliet*
Emlyn Williams, A *Boy Growing Up*

LEADING ACTRESS (PLAY)

Wendy Hiller, A *Moon for the Misbegotten*
Eugenie Leontovich, T*he Cave Dwellers*
☆ Helen Hayes, T*ime Remembered*
Siobhan McKenna, T*he Rope Dancers*
Mary Ure, L*ook Back in Anger*
Jo Van Fleet, L*ook Homeward, Angel*

FEATURED ACTOR (PLAY)
Sig Arno, *Time Remembered*
Theodore Bikel, *The Rope Dancers*
Pat Hingle, *The Dark at the Top of the Stairs*
☆ Henry Jones, *Sunrise at Campobello*
George Relph, *The Entertainer*

FEATURED ACTRESS (PLAY)
☆ Anne Bancroft, *Two for the Seesaw*
Brenda de Banzie, *The Entertainer*
Joan Blondell, *The Rope Dancers*
Mary Fickett, *Sunrise at Campobello*
Eileen Heckart, *The Dark at the Top of the Stairs*

LEADING ACTOR (MUSICAL)
Ricardo Montalban, *Jamaica*
☆ Robert Preston, *The Music Man*
Eddie Foy, Jr., *Rumple*
Tony Randall, *Oh, Captain!*

LEADING ACTRESS (MUSICAL)
☆ Thelma Ritter, *New Girl in Town*
Lena Horne, *Jamaica*
Beatrice Lillie, *Ziegfeld Follies*
☆ Gwen Verdon, *New Girl in Town*

FEATURED ACTOR (MUSICAL)
☆ David Burns, *The Music Man*
Ossie Davis, *Jamaica*
Cameron Prud'homme, *New Girl in Town*
Iggie Wolfington, *The Music Man*

FEATURED ACTRESS (MUSICAL)
☆ Barbara Cook, *The Music Man*
Susan Johnson, *Oh, Captain!*
Carol Lawrence, *West Side Story*
Jacquelyn McKeever, *Oh, Captain!*
Josephine Premice, *Jamaica*

AUTHOR (PLAY)
☆ Dore Schary, *Sunrise at Campobello*

PRODUCERS (PLAY)
☆ Lawrence Langner, Theresa Helburn, Armina Marshall, and
Dore Schary, *Sunrise at Campobello*

DIRECTOR (PLAY)
☆   Vincent J. Donehue, *Sunrise at Campobello*
Morton da Costa, *The Music Man*
Peter Hall, *The Rope Dancers*
George Roy Hill, *Look Homeward, Angel*
Elia Kazan, *The Dark at the Top of the Stairs*
Arthur Penn, *Two for the Seesaw*

AUTHOR (MUSICAL)
☆   Meredith Willson and Franklin Lacey, *The Music Man*

PRODUCER (MUSICAL)
☆   Kermit Bloomgarden, Herbert Greene and Frank
      Productions, *The Music Man*

COMPOSER AND LYRICIST
☆   Meredith Willson, *The Music Man*

SCENIC DESIGNER
Boris Aronson, *Orpheus Descending* / *A Hole in the Head* / *The Rope
      Dancers*
Ben Edwards, *The Dark at the Top of the Stairs*
Peter Larkin, *Look Homeward, Angel* / *Miss Lonelyhearts* / *The Square
      Root of Wonderful* / *Oh, Captain!* / *The Day the Money Stopped*
☆   Oliver Smith, *Brigadoon* / *Carousel* / *Jamaica* / *Nude with Violin* /
      Time Remembered / ☆ *West Side Story*

COSTUME DESIGNER
Lucinda Ballard, *Orpheus Descending*
☆   Motley, *Look Back in Anger* / *Look Homeward, Angel* / *Shinebone
      Alley* / *The Country Wife* / ☆ *The First Gentleman*
Irene Sharaff, *West Side Story*
Miles White, *Jamaica* / *Time Remembered* / *Oh, Captain!*

CHOREOGRAPHER
Bob Fosse, *New Girl in Town*
☆   Jerome Robbins, *West Side Story*
Onna White, *The Music Man*

CONDUCTOR AND MUSICAL DIRECTOR
☆   Herbert Greene, *The Music Man*
Max Goberman, *West Side Story*

STAGE TECHNICIAN
☆   Harry Romar, *Time Remembered*
Sammy Knapp, *The Music Man*

SPECIAL AWARDS
☆ Circle in the Square
☆ Phoenix Theatre
☆ New York Shakespeare Festival, for presenting in Central Park and the Hecksher Theater.
☆ Mrs. Martin Beck, for fifteen years of untiring dedication to the American Theatre Wing, which she served as treasurer, secretary and chairman of the board of directors.
☆ Esther Hawley

1959

MUSICAL
Flower Drum Song. Music by Richard Rodgers, lyrics by Oscar Hammerstein II, book by Oscar Hammerstein II, and Joseph Fields. Produced by Joseph Fields, Oscar Hammerstein II, and Richard Rodgers.
La Plume de Ma Tante. Written, devised, and directed by Robert Dhéry, music by Gerard Calvi, English lyrics by Ross Parker. David Merrick and Joseph Kipness present the Jack Hylton Production.
☆ *Redhead*. Music by Albert Hague, lyrics by Dorothy Fields, book by Herbert and Dorothy Fields, Sidney Sheldon and David Shaw. Produced by Robert Fryer and Lawrence Carr.

PLAY
A Touch of the Poet by Eugene O'Neill. Produced by The Producers Theatre, Robert Whitehead, and Roger L. Stevens.
Epitaph for George Dillon by John Osborne and Anthony Creighton. Produced by David Merrick and Joshua Logan.
☆ *J.B.* by Archibald MacLeish. Produced by Alfred de Liagre, Jr.
The Disenchanted by Budd Schulberg and Harvey Breit. Produced by William Darrid and Eleanor Saidenberg.
The Visit by Friedrich Duerrenmatt, adapted by Maurice Valency. Produced by The Producers Theatre.

LEADING ACTOR (PLAY)
Cedric Hardwicke, *A Majority of One*
Alfred Lunt, *The Visit*
Christopher Plummer, *J.B.*
Cyril Ritchard, *The Pleasure of His Company*
☆ Jason Robards, Jr., *The Disenchanted*
Robert Stevens, *Epitaph for George Dillon*

LEADING ACTRESS (PLAY)
☆ Gertrude Berg, A *Majority of One*
Claudette Colbert, *The Marriage-Go-Round*
Lynn Fontanne, *The Visit*
Kim Stanley, A *Touch of the Poet*
Maureen Stapleton, *The Cold Wind and the Warm*

FEATURED ACTOR (PLAY)
Marc Connelly, *Tall Story*
George Grizzard, *The Disenchanted*
Walter Matthau, *Once More, with Feeling*
Robert Morse, *Say, Darling*
☆ Charlie Ruggles, *The Pleasure of His Company*
George C. Scott, *Comes a Day*

FEATURED ACTRESS (PLAY)
Maureen Delany, *God and Kate Murphy*
Dolores Hart, *The Pleasure of His Company*
☆ Julie Newmar, *The Marriage-Go-Round*
Nan Martin, *J.B.*
Beatrice Reading, *Requiem for a Nun*

LEADING ACTOR (MUSICAL)
Larry Blyden, *Flower Drum Song*
☆ Richard Kiley, *Redhead*

LEADING ACTRESS (MUSICAL)
Miyoshi Umeki, *Flower Drum Song*
☆ Gwen Verdon, *Redhead*

FEATURED ACTOR (MUSICAL)
☆ Russell Nype, *Goldilocks*
☆ Leonard Stone, *Redhead*

FEATURED ACTRESS (MUSICAL)
Julienne Marie, *Whoop-Up*
☆ Pat Stanley, *Goldilocks*

AUTHOR (PLAY)
☆ Archibald MacLeish, *J.B.*

PRODUCER (PLAY)
☆ Alfred de Liagre, Jr., *J.B.*

DIRECTOR
Peter Brook, *The Visit*
Robert Dhéry, *La Plume de Ma Tante*
William Gaskill, *Epitaph for George Dillon*

Peter Glenville, *Rashomon*
☆ Elia Kazan, J.B.
Cyril Ritchard, *The Pleasure of His Company*
Dore Schary, *A Majority of One*

AUTHORS (MUSICAL)
☆ Herbert and Dorothy Fields, Sidney Sheldon and David Shaw, *Redhead*

PRODUCERS (MUSICAL)
☆ Robert Fryer and Lawrence Carr, *Redhead*

COMPOSER
☆ Albert Hague, *Redhead*

CONDUCTOR AND MUSICAL DIRECTOR
Jay Blackston, *Redhead*
☆ Salvatore Dell'Isola, *Flower Drum Song*
Lehman Engel, *Goldilocks*
Gershon Kingsley, *La Plume de Ma Tante*

SCENIC DESIGNER
Boris Aronson, J.B.
Ballou, *The Legend of Lizzie*
Ben Edwards, *Jane Eyre*
Oliver Messel, *Rashomon*
☆ Donald Oenslager, *A Majority of One*
Teo Otto, *The Visit*

COSTUME DESIGNER
Castillo, *Goldilocks*
Dorothy Jeakins, *The World of Suzie Wong*
Oliver Messel, *Rashomon*
Irene Sharaff, *Flower Drum Song*
☆ Rouben Ter-Arutunian, *Redhead*

CHOREOGRAPHER
Agnes de Mille, *Goldilocks*
☆ Bob Fosse, *Redhead*
Carol Haney, *Flower Drum Song*
Onna White, *Whoop-Up*

STAGE TECHNICIAN
Thomas Fitzgerald, *Who Was That Lady I Saw You With?*
Edward Flynn, *The Most Happy Fella* (City Center Revival)
☆ Sam Knapp, *The Music Man*

SPECIAL AWARDS

☆ John Gielgud, for contribution to theatre for his extraordinary insight into the writings of Shakespeare as demonstrated in his one-man play, *Ages of Man*.

☆ Howard Lindsey and Russel Crouse, for a collaboration that lasted longer than Gilbert and Sullivan.

☆ Cast of *La Plume de Ma Tante* (Pamela Austin, Colette Brosset, Roger Caccia, Yvonne Constant, Genevieve Coulombel, Robert Dhéry, Michael Kent, Jean Lefevre, Jaques Legras, Michel Modo, Pierre Olaf, Nicole Parent, Ross Parker, and Henri Pennec) for contribution to the theatre.

The 1960s

"There is something very special about having
your work acknowledged by your peers. It is a mile-
stone to work for, and the 'first time' like this happens
to you it is deeply satisfying."

Joel Grey
Featured Actor (Musical), *Cabaret*

"The curious thing about awards is that one receives
them for work one does not expect to receive them for,
and does not receive them for work one does. For
instance, I received the Tony for 'Hallelujah, Baby!'—
and not for 'Gypsy!' But, the Tony, which stands for
excellence in the theatre, is an honor wherever it
comes!"

Jule Styne
Score, *Hallelujah, Baby!*

MARY MARTIN, JACKIE GLEASON, ANNE BANCROFT,
AND MELVYN DOUGLAS *at the 1960 Tony Awards.*

1960

MUSICAL

☆ *Fiorello!* Music by Jerry Bock, lyrics by Sheldon Harnick, book by Jerome Weidman and George Abbott. Produced by Robert E. Griffith and Harold S. Prince.

Gypsy. Music by Jule Styne, lyrics by Stephen Sondheim, book by Arthur Laurents. Produced by David Merrick and Leland Hayward.

Once Upon a Mattress. Music by Mary Rodgers, lyrics by Marshall Barer, book by Jay Thompson, Marshall Barer, and Dean Fuller. Produced by T. Edward Hambleton, Norris Houghton, and William and Jean Eckart.

Take Me Along. Music and lyrics by Bob Merrill, book by Joseph Stein and Robert Russell. Produced by David Merrick.

☆ *The Sound of Music.* Music by Richard Rodgers, lyrics by Oscar Hammerstein II, book by Howard Lindsay and Russel Crouse. Produced by Leland Hayward, Richard Halliday, and Rodgers and Hammerstein.

PLAY

A Raisin in the Sun by Lorraine Hansberry. Produced by Philip Rose and David J. Cogan.

The Best Man by Gore Vidal. Produced by The Playwrights' Company.

☆ *The Miracle Worker* by William Gibson. Produced by Fred Coe.

The Tenth Man by Paddy Chayefsky. Produced by Saint-Subber and Arthur Cantor.

Toys in the Attic by Lillian Hellman. Produced by Kermit Bloomgarden.

LEADING ACTOR (PLAY)

☆ Melvyn Douglas, *The Best Man*
Lee Tracy, *The Best Man*
Jason Robards, Jr., *Toys in the Attic*
Sidney Poitier, *A Raisin in the Sun*
George C. Scott, *The Andersonville Trial*

LEADING ACTRESS (PLAY)

☆ Anne Bancroft, *The Miracle Worker*
Margaret Leighton, *Much Ado About Nothing*
Claudia McNeil, *A Raisin in the Sun*
Geraldine Page, *Sweet Bird of Youth*
Maureen Stapleton, *Toys in the Attic*
Irene Worth, *Toys in the Attic*

FEATURED ACTOR (PLAY)
Warren Beatty, A *Loss of Roses*
Harry Guardino, *One More River*
☆ Roddy McDowall, *The Fighting Cock*
Rip Torn, *Sweet Bird of Youth*
Lawrence Winters, *The Long Dream*

FEATURED ACTRESS (PLAY)
Leora Dana, *The Best Man*
Jane Fonda, *There Was a Little Girl*
Sarah Marshall, *Goodbye, Charlie*
Juliet Mills, *Five Finger Exercise*
☆ Anne Revere, *Toys in the Attic*

LEADING ACTOR (MUSICAL)
☆ Jackie Gleason, *Take Me Along*
Robert Morse, *Take Me Along*
Walter Pidgeon, *Take Me Along*
Andy Griffith, *Destry Rides Again*
Anthony Perkins, *Greenwillow*

LEADING ACTRESS (MUSICAL)
Carol Burnett, *Once Upon a Mattress*
Dolores Gray, *Destry Rides Again*
Eileen Herlie, *Take Me Along*
☆ Mary Martin, *The Sound of Music*
Ethel Merman, *Gypsy*

FEATURED ACTOR (MUSICAL)
Theodore Bikel, *The Sound of Music*
Kurt Kasznar, *The Sound of Music*
☆ Tom Bosley, *Fiorello!*
Howard Da Silva, *Fiorello!*
Jack Klugman, *Gypsy*

FEATURED ACTRESS (MUSICAL)
Sandra Church, *Gypsy*
Pert Kelton, *Greenwillow*
☆ Patricia Neway, *The Sound of Music*
Lauri Peters, *The Sound of Music*
The Children (Kathy Dunn, Evanna Lien, Mary Susan Locke,
    Marilyn Robers, William Snowden, and Joseph Stewart),
    The Sound of Music

AUTHOR (PLAY)
☆ William Gibson, *The Miracle Worker*

PRODUCER (PLAY)
☆ Fred Coe, *The Miracle Worker*

DIRECTOR (PLAY)
Joseph Anthony, *The Best Man*
Tyrone Guthrie, *The Tenth Man*
Elia Kazan, *Sweet Bird of Youth*
☆ Arthur Penn, *The Miracle Worker*
Lloyd Richards, A *Raisin in the Sun*

AUTHORS (MUSICAL)
☆ Jerome Weidman and George Abbott, *Fiorello!*
☆ Howard Lindsay and Russel Crouse, *The Sound of Music*

PRODUCER (MUSICAL)
☆ Robert E. Griffith and Harold S. Prince, *Fiorello!*
☆ Leland Hayward and Richard Halliday, *The Sound of Music*

DIRECTOR (MUSICAL)
☆ George Abbott, *Fiorello!*
Vincent J. Donehue, *The Sound of Music*
Peter Glenville, *Take Me Along*
Michael Kidd, *Destry Rides Again*
Jerome Robbins, *Gypsy*

COMPOSERS
☆ Jerry Bock, *Fiorello!*
☆ Richard Rodgers, *The Sound of Music*

CONDUCTOR AND MUSICAL DIRECTOR
Abba Bogin, *Greenwillow*
☆ Frederick Dvonch, *The Sound of Music*
Lehman Engel, *Take Me Along*
Hal Hastings, *Fiorello!*
Milton Rosenstock, *Gypsy*

SCENIC DESIGNER (PLAY)
Will Steven Armstrong, *Caligula*
☆ Howard Bay, *Toys in the Attic*
David Hays, *The Tenth Man*
George Jenkins, *The Miracle Worker*
Jo Mielziner, *The Best Man*

SCENIC DESIGNER (MUSICAL)
Cecil Beaton, *Saratoga*
William and Jean Eckart, *Fiorello!*
Peter Larkin, *Greenwillow*

Jo Mielziner, *Gypsy*
☆ Oliver Smith, *The Sound of Music*

COSTUME DESIGNER
☆ Cecil Beaton, *Saratoga*
Alvin Colt, *Greenwillow*
Raoul Pène du Bois, *Gypsy*
Miles White, *Take Me Along*

CHOREOGRAPHER
Peter Gennaro, *Fiorello!*
☆ Michael Kidd, *Destry Rides Again*
Joe Layton, *Greenwillow*
Lee Scott, *Happy Town*
Onna White, *Take Me Along*

STAGE TECHNICIAN
Al Alloy, chief electrician, *Take Me Along*
James Orr, chief electrician, *Greenwillow*
☆ John Walters, chief carpenter, *The Miracle Worker*

SPECIAL AWARDS
☆ John D. Rockefeller III, for vision and leadership in creating
    the Lincoln Center, a landmark of theatre encompassing
    the performing arts.
☆ James Thurber and Burgess Meredith, *A Thurber Carnival*

1961

MUSICAL
☆ *Bye Bye Birdie*. Music by Charles Strouse, lyrics by Lee
    Adams, book by Michael Stewart. Produced by Edward
    Padula in association with L. Slade Brown.
Do Re Mi. Music by Jules Styne, lyrics by Betty Comden and
    Adolph Green, book by Garson Kanin. Produced by David
    Merrick.
Irma la Douce. Music by Marguerite Monnot, book and lyrics by
    Alexandre Breffort. English book and lyrics by Julian
    More, David Heneker and Monty Norman. Produced by
    David Merrick in association with Donald Albery, and
    H.M. Tennent, Ltd.

PLAY
All the Way Home by Tad Mosel. Produced by Fred Coe in association with Arthur Cantor.

☆ *Becket* by Jean Anouilh, translated by Lucienne Hill.
   Produced by David Merrick.
The Devil's Advocate by Dore Schary. Produced by Dore Schary.
The Hostage by Brendan Behan. Produced by S. Field and
   Caroline Burke Swann.

LEADING ACTOR (PLAY)
Hume Cronyn, *Big Fish, Little Fish*
Sam Levene, *The Devil's Advocate*
☆ Zero Mostel, *Rhinoceros*
Anthony Quinn, *Becket*

LEADING ACTRESS (PLAY)
Tallulah Bankhead, *Midgie Purvis*
Barbara Baxley, *Period of Adjustment*
Barbara Bel Geddes, *Mary, Mary*
☆ Joan Plowright, *A Taste of Honey*

FEATURED ACTOR (PLAY)
Philip Bosco, *The Rape of the Belt*
Eduardo Ciannelli, *The Devil's Advocate*
☆ Martin Gabel, *Big Fish, Little Fish*
George Grizzard, *Big Fish, Little Fish*

FEATURED ACTRESS (PLAY)
☆ Colleen Dewhurst, *All the Way Home*
Eileen Heckart, *Invitation to a March*
Tresa Hughes, *The Devil's Advocate*
Rosemary Murphy, *Period of Adjustment*

LEADING ACTOR (MUSICAL)
☆ Richard Burton, *Camelot*
Phil Silvers, *Do Re Mi*
Maurice Evans, *Tenderloin*

LEADING ACTRESS (MUSICAL)
Julie Andrews, *Camelot*
Carol Channing, *Show Girl*
☆ Elizabeth Seal, *Irma la Douce*
Nancy Walker, *Do Re Mi*

FEATURED ACTOR (MUSICAL)
Clive Revill, *Irma la Douce*
Dick Gautier, *Bye Bye Birdie*
Ron Husmann, *Tenderloin*
☆ Dick Van Dyke, *Bye Bye Birdie*

FEATURED ACTRESS (MUSICAL)
Nancy Dussault, Do Re Mi
☆ Tammy Grimes, The Unsinkable Molly Brown
Chita Rivera, Bye Bye Birdie

AUTHOR (PLAY)
☆ Jean Anouilh, Becket

PRODUCER (PLAY)
☆ David Merrick, Becket

DIRECTOR (PLAY)
Joseph Anthony, Rhinoceros
☆ Sir John Gielgud, Big Fish, Little Fish
Joan Littlewood, The Hostage
Arthur Penn, All the Way Home

AUTHOR (MUSICAL)
☆ Michael Stewart, Bye Bye Birdie

PRODUCER (MUSICAL)
☆ Edward Padula, Bye Bye Birdie

DIRECTOR (MUSICAL)
Peter Brook, Irma la Douce
☆ Gower Champion, Bye Bye Birdie
Garson Kanin, Do Re Mi

CONDUCTOR AND MUSICAL DIRECTOR
☆ Franz Allers, Camelot
Pembroke Davenport, 13 Daughters
Stanley Lebowsky, Irma la Douce
Elliot Lawrence, Bye Bye Birdie

SCENIC DESIGNER (PLAY)
Roger Furse, Duel of Angels
David Hays, All the Way Home
Jo Mielziner, The Devil's Advocate
☆ Oliver Smith, Becket
Rouben Ter-Arutunian, Advise and Consent

SCENIC DESIGNER (MUSICAL)
George Jenkins, 13 Daughters
Robert Randolph, Bye Bye Birdie
☆ Oliver Smith, Camelot

COSTUME DESIGNER (PLAY)
Theoni V. Aldredge, The Devil's Advocate

☆ Motley, *Becket*
Raymond Sovey, *All the Way Home*

COSTUME DESIGNER (MUSICAL)
☆ Adrian and Tony Duquette, *Camelot*
Rolf Gerard, *Irma la Douce*
Cecil Beaton, *Tenderloin*

CHOREOGRAPHER
☆ Gower Champion, *Bye Bye Birdie*
Onna White, *Irma la Douce*

STAGE TECHNICIAN
☆ Teddy Van Bemmel, *Becket*

SPECIAL AWARDS
☆ David Merrick, in recognition of a fabulous production record over the last seven years.
☆ The Theatre Guild, for organizing the first repertory to go abroad for the State Department.

1962

MUSICAL
Carnival. Music and lyrics by Bob Merrill, book by Michael Stewart and Helen Deutsch. Produced by David Merrick.
☆ *How to Succeed in Business Without Really Trying.* Music and lyrics by Frank Loesser, book by Abe Burrows, Jack Weinstock and Willie Gilbert. Produced by Cy Feuer and Ernest Martin.
Milk and Honey. Lyrics and music by Jerry Herman, book by Don Appell. Produced by Gerard Oestreicher.
No Strings. Music and lyrics by Richard Rodgers, book by Samuel Taylor. Produced by Richard Rodgers in association with Samuel Taylor.

PLAY
☆ *A Man for All Seasons* by Robert Bolt. Produced by Robert Whitehead and Roger L. Stevens.
Gideon by Paddy Chayefsky. Produced by Fred Coe and Arthur Cantor.
The Caretaker by Harold Pinter. Produced by Roger L. Stevens, Frederick Brisson, and Gilbert Miller.
The Night of the Iguana by Tennessee Williams. Produced by Charles Bowden and Viola Rubber.

LEADING ACTOR (PLAY)
Fredric March, *Gideon*
John Mills, *Ross*
Donald Pleasence, *The Caretaker*
☆ Paul Scofield, *A Man for All Seasons*

LEADING ACTRESS (PLAY)
Gladys Cooper, *A Passage to India*
Colleen Dewhurst, *Great Day in the Morning*
☆ Margaret Leighton, *The Night of the Iguana*
Kim Stanley, *A Far Country*

FEATURED ACTOR (PLAY)
Godfrey M. Cambridge, *Purlie Victorious*
Joseph Campanella, *A Gift of Time*
☆ Walter Matthau, *A Shot in the Dark*
Paul Sparer, *Ross*

FEATURED ACTRESS (PLAY)
☆ Elizabeth Ashley, *Take Her, She's Mine*
Zohra Lampert, *Look: We've Come Through*
Janet Margolin, *Daughter of Silence*
Pat Stanley, *Sunday in New York*

LEADING ACTOR (MUSICAL)
Ray Bolger, *All American*
Alfred Drake, *Kismet*
Richard Kiley, *No Strings*
☆ Robert Morse, *How to Succeed in Business Without Really Trying*

LEADING ACTRESS (MUSICAL)
☆ Anna Maria Alberghetti, *Carnival*
☆ Diahann Carroll, *No Strings*
Molly Picon, *Milk and Honey*
Elaine Stritch, *Sail Away*

FEATURED ACTOR (MUSICAL)
Orson Bean, *Subways Are for Sleeping*
Severn Darden, *From the Second City*
Pierre Olaf, *Carnival*
☆ Charles Nelson Reilly, *How to Succeed in Business Without Really Trying*

FEATURED ACTRESS (MUSICAL)
Elizabeth Allen, *The Gay Life*
Barbara Harris, *From the Second City*

☆   Phyllis Newman, *Subways Are for Sleeping*

Barbra Streisand, *I Can Get It for You Wholesale*

AUTHOR (PLAY)

☆   Robert Bolt, *A Man for All Seasons*

PRODUCER (PLAY)

Charles Bowden and Viola Rubber, *The Night of the Iguana*

Fred Coe and Arthur Cantor, *Gideon*

David Merrick, *Ross*

☆   Robert Whitehead and Roger L. Stevens, *A Man for All Seasons*

DIRECTOR (PLAY)

Tyrone Guthrie, *Gideon*

Donald McWhinnie, *The Caretaker*

José Quintero, *Great Day in the Morning*

☆   Noel Willman, *A Man for All Seasons*

AUTHOR (MUSICAL)

☆   Abe Burrows, Jack Weinstock and Willie Gilbert, *How to Succeed in Business Without Really Trying*

Michael Stewart and Helen Deutsch, *Carnival*

PRODUCER (MUSICAL)

Helen Bonfils, Haila Stoddard and Charles Russell, *Sail Away*

☆   Cy Feuer and Ernest Martin, *How to Succeed in Business Without Really Trying*

David Merrick, *Carnival*

Gerard Oestreicher, *Milk and Honey*

DIRECTOR (MUSICAL)

☆   Abe Burrows, *How to Succeed in Business Without Really Trying*

Gower Champion, *Carnival*

Joe Layton, *No Strings*

Joshua Logan, *All American*

COMPOSER

Richard Adler, *Kwamina*

Jerry Herman, *Milk and Honey*

Frank Loesser, *How to Succeed in Business Without Really Trying*

☆   Richard Rodgers, *No Strings*

CONDUCTOR AND MUSICAL DIRECTOR

Pembroke Davenport, *Kean*

Herbert Greene, *The Gay Life*

☆   Elliot Lawrence, *How to Succeed in Business Without Really Trying*

Peter Matz, *No Strings*

SCENIC DESIGNER
☆ Will Steven Armstrong, *Carnival*
Rouben Ter-Arutunian, A *Passage to India*
David Hays, N*o Strings*
Oliver Smith, T*he Gay Life*

COSTUME DESIGNER
☆ Lucinda Ballard, T*he Gay Life*
Donald Brooks, N*o Strings*
Motley, *Kwamina*
Miles White, *Milk and Honey*

CHOREOGRAPHER
☆ Agnes de Mille, *Kwamina*
Michael Kidd, *Subways Are for Sleeping*
Dania Krupska, T*he Happiest Girl in the World*
☆ Joe Layton, N*o Strings*

STAGE TECHNICIAN
Al Alloy, *Ross*
☆ Michael Burns, A *Man for All Seasons*

SPECIAL AWARDS
☆ Brooks Atkinson
☆ Franco Zeffirelli, for designs and direction of the Old Vic's
Romeo and Juliet.
☆ Richard Rodgers, for all he has done for young people in the
theatre and "for taking the men of the orchestra out of the
pit and putting them on stage" in N*o Strings.*

1963

MUSICAL
☆ A F*unny Thing Happened on the Way to the Forum.* Music and
lyrics by Stephen Sondheim, book by Burt Shevelove and
Larry Gelbart. Produced by Harold Prince.
Little Me. Music by Cy Coleman, lyrics by Carolyn Leigh, book by
Neil Simon. Produced by Cy Feuer and Ernest Martin.
Oliver! Music, lyrics, and book by Lionel Bart. Produced by David
Merrick and Donald Albery.
Stop the World—I Want to Get Off. Music, lyrics, and book by Leslie
Bricusse and Anthony Newley. Produced by David
Merrick in association with Bernard Delfont.

PLAY

A *Thousand Clowns* by Herb Gardner. Produced by Fred Coe and
Arthur Cantor.

Mother Courage and Her Children by Bertolt Brecht, adapted by Eric
Bentley. Produced by Cheryl Crawford and Jerome
Robbins.

Tchin-Tchin by Sidney Michaels. Produced by David Merrick.

☆ *Who's Afraid of Virginia Woolf?* by Edward Albee. Produced by
Theatre 1963, Richard Barr, and Clinton Wilder.

LEADING ACTOR (PLAY)

Charles Boyer, *Lord Pengo*
Paul Ford, *Never Too Late*
☆ Arthur Hill, *Who's Afraid of Virginia Woolf?*
Bert Lahr, *The Beauty Part*

LEADING ACTRESS (PLAY)

Hermione Baddeley, *The Milk Train Doesn't Stop Here Anymore*
☆ Uta Hagen, *Who's Afraid of Virginia Woolf?*
Margaret Leighton, *Tchin-Tchin*
Claudia McNeill, *Tiger Tiger Burning Bright*

FEATURED ACTOR (PLAY)

☆ Alan Arkin, *Enter Laughing*
Barry Gordon, *A Thousand Clowns*
Paul Rogers, *Photo Finish*
Frank Silvera, *The Lady of the Camellias*

FEATURED ACTRESS (PLAY)

☆ Sandy Dennis, *A Thousand Clowns*
Melinda Dillon, *Who's Afraid of Virginia Woolf?*
Alice Ghostley, *The Beauty Part*
Zohra Lampert, *Mother Courage and Her Children*

LEADING ACTOR (MUSICAL)

Sid Caesar, *Little Me*
☆ Zero Mostel, *A Funny Thing Happened on the Way to the Forum*
Anthony Newley, *Stop the World—I Want to Get Off*
Clive Revill, *Oliver!*

LEADING ACTRESS (MUSICAL)

Georgia Brown, *Oliver!*
Nanette Fabray, *Mr. President*
Sally Ann Howes, *Brigadoon*
☆ Vivien Leigh, *Tovarich*

FEATURED ACTOR (MUSICAL)
☆ David Burns, A *Funny Thing Happened on the Way to the Forum*
Jack Gilford, A *Funny Thing Happened on the Way to the Forum*
David Jones, *Oliver!*
Swen Swenson, *Little Me*

FEATURED ACTRESS (MUSICAL)
Ruth Kobart, A *Funny Thing Happened on the Way to the Forum*
Virginia Martin, *Little Me*
☆ Anna Quayle, *Stop the World—I Want to Get Off*
Louise Troy, *Tovarich*

PRODUCER (PLAY)
The Actors Studio Theatre, *Strange Interlude*
☆ Clinton Wilder and Richard Barr, Theatre 1963, *Who's Afraid of Virginia Woolf?*
Cheryl Crawford and Jerome Robbins, *Mother Courage and Her Children*
Paul Vroom, Buff Cobb, and Burry Fredrik, *Too True To Be Good*

DIRECTOR (PLAY)
George Abbott, *Never Too Late*
John Gielgud, *The School for Scandal*
Peter Glenville, *Tchin-Tchin*
☆ Alan Schneider, *Who's Afraid of Virginia Woolf?*

AUTHOR (MUSICAL)
Lionel Bart, *Oliver!*
Leslie Bricusse and Anthony Newley, *Stop the World—I Want to Get Off*
☆ Burt Shevelove and Larry Gelbart, A *Funny Thing Happened on the Way to the Forum*
Neil Simon, *Little Me*

PRODUCER (MUSICAL)
Cy Feuer and Ernest Martin, *Little Me*
David Merrick and Donald Albery, *Oliver!*
☆ Harold Prince, A *Funny Thing Happened on the Way to the Forum*

DIRECTOR (MUSICAL)
☆ George Abbott, A *Funny Thing Happened on the Way to the Forum*
Peter Coe, *Oliver!*
John Fearnley, *Brigadoon*
Cy Feuer and Bob Fosse, *Little Me*

COMPOSER AND LYRICIST
☆ Lionel Bart, *Oliver!*
Leslie Bricusse and Anthony Newley, *Stop the World—I Want to Get Off*
Cy Coleman and Carolyn Leigh, *Little Me*
Milton Schafer and Ronny Graham, *Bravo Giovanni*

CONDUCTOR AND MUSICAL DIRECTOR
Jay Blackton, *Mr. President*
Anton Coppola, *Bravo Giovanni*
☆ Donald Pippin, *Oliver!*
Julius Rudel, *Brigadoon*

SCENIC DESIGNER
Will Steven Armstrong, *Tchin-Tchin*
☆ Sean Kenny, *Oliver!*
Anthony Powell, *The School for Scandal*
Franco Zeffirelli, *The Lady of the Camellias*

COSTUME DESIGNER
Marcel Escoffier, *The Lady of the Camellias*
Robert Fletcher, *Little Me*
Motley, *Mother Courage and Her Children*
☆ Anthony Powell, *The School for Scandal*

CHOREOGRAPHER
☆ Bob Fosse, *Little Me*
Carol Haney, *Bravo Giovanni*

STAGE TECHNICIAN
☆ Solly Pernick, *Mr. President*
Milton Smith, *Beyond the Fringe*

SPECIAL AWARDS
☆ W. McNeil Lowry, on behalf of the Ford Foundation for his and their distinguished support of the American Theatre.
☆ Irving Berlin, for his distinguished contribution to the musical theatre for these many years.
☆ Alan Bennett, Peter Cook, Jonathan Miller, Dudley Moore, *Beyond the Fringe*, for their brilliance which has shattered all the old concepts of comedy.

1964

MUSICAL

Funny Girl. Music by Jule Styne, lyrics by Bob Merrill, book by Isobel Lennart. Produced by Ray Stark.

☆ *Hello, Dolly!* Music and lyrics by Jerry Herman, book by Michael Stewart. Produced by David Merrick.

High Spirits. Music, lyrics, and book by Hugh Martin and Timothy Gray. Produced by Lester Osterman, Robert Fletcher, and Richard Horner.

She Loves Me. Music by Jerry Bock, lyrics by Sheldon Harnick, book by Joe Masteroff. Produced by Harold Prince in association with Lawrence N. Kasha and Philip C. McKenna.

PLAY

The Ballad of the Sad Café by Edward Albee. Produced by Lewis Allen and Ben Edwards.

Barefoot in the Park by Neil Simon. Produced by Saint-Subber.

Dylan by Sidney Michaels. Produced by George W. George and Frank Granat.

☆ *Luther* by John Osborne. Produced by David Merrick.

LEADING ACTOR (PLAY)

Richard Burton, *Hamlet*
Albert Finney, *Luther*
☆ Alec Guinness, *Dylan*
Jason Robards, Jr., *After the Fall*

LEADING ACTRESS (PLAY)

Elizabeth Ashley, *Barefoot in the Park*
☆ Sandy Dennis, *Any Wednesday*
Colleen Dewhurst, *The Ballad of the Sad Café*
Julie Harris, *Marathon '33*

FEATURED ACTOR (PLAY)

Lee Allen, *Marathon '33*
☆ Hume Cronyn, *Hamlet*
Michael Dunn, *The Ballad of the Sad Café*
Larry Gates, *A Case of Libel*

FEATURED ACTRESS (PLAY)

☆ Barbara Loden, *After the Fall*
Rosemary Murphy, *Any Wednesday*
Kate Reid, *Dylan*
Diana Sands, *Blues for Mister Charlie*

Photo: Anita and Steve Shevett

CAROL CHANNING

LEADING ACTOR (MUSICAL)
Sydney Chaplin, *Funny Girl*
Bob Fosse, *Pal Joey* (City Center Revival)
☆ Bert Lahr, *Foxy*
Steve Lawrence, *What Makes Sammy Run?*

LEADING ACTRESS (MUSICAL)
☆ Carol Channing, *Hello, Dolly!*
Beatrice Lillie, *High Spirits*
Barbra Streisand, *Funny Girl*
Inga Swenson, *110 in the Shade*

FEATURED ACTOR (MUSICAL)
☆ Jack Cassidy, *She Loves Me*
Will Geer, *110 in the Shade*
Danny Meehan, *Funny Girl*
Charles Nelson Reilly, *Hello, Dolly!*

FEATURED ACTRESS (MUSICAL)
Julienne Marie, *Foxy*
Kay Medford, *Funny Girl*
☆ Tessie O'Shea, *The Girl Who Came to Supper*
Louise Troy, *High Spirits*

AUTHOR (PLAY)
☆ John Osborne, *Luther*

PRODUCER (PLAY)
Lewis Allen and Ben Edwards, *The Ballad of the Sad Café*
George W. George and Frank Granat, *Dylan*
☆ Herman Shumlin, *The Deputy*
Saint-Subber, *Barefoot in the Park*

DIRECTOR (PLAY)
June Havoc, *Marathon '33*
☆ Mike Nichols, *Barefoot in the Park*
Alan Schneider, *The Ballad of the Sad Café*
Herman Shumlin, *The Deputy*

AUTHOR (MUSICAL)
Noel Coward and Harry Kurnitz, *The Girl Who Came to Supper*
Joe Masteroff, *She Loves Me*
Hugh Martin and Timothy Gray, *High Spirits*
☆ Michael Stewart, *Hello, Dolly!*

PRODUCER (MUSICAL)
City Center Light Opera Company, *West Side Story*
☆ David Merrick, *Hello, Dolly!*
Harold Prince, *She Loves Me*
Ray Stark, *Funny Girl*

DIRECTOR (MUSICAL)
Joseph Anthony, *110 in the Shade*

☆ Gower Champion, *Hello, Dolly!*
Noel Coward, *High Spirits*
Harold Prince, *She Loves Me*

COMPOSER AND LYRICIST
☆ Jerry Herman, *Hello, Dolly!*
Hugh Martin and Timothy Gray, *High Spirits*
Harvey Schmidt and Tom Jones, *110 in the Shade*
Jule Styne and Bob Merrill, *Funny Girl*

CONDUCTOR AND MUSICAL DIRECTOR
☆ Shepard Coleman, *Hello, Dolly!*
Lehman Engel, *What Makes Sammy Run?*
Charles Jaffe, *West Side Story*
Fred Werner, *High Spirits*

SCENIC DESIGNER
Raoul Pène du Bois, *The Student Gypsy*
Ben Edwards, *The Ballad of the Sad Café*
David Hays, *Marco Millions*
☆ Oliver Smith, *Hello, Dolly!*

COSTUME DESIGNER
Irene Sharaff, *The Girl Who Came to Supper*
Beni Montresor, *Marco Millions*
Rouben Ter-Arutunian, *Arturo Ui*
☆ Freddy Wittop, *Hello, Dolly!*

CHOREOGRAPHER
☆ Gower Champion, *Hello, Dolly!*
Danny Daniels, *High Spirits*
Carol Haney, *Funny Girl*
Herbert Ross, *Anyone Can Whistle*

SPECIAL AWARD
☆ Eva Le Gallienne, celebrating her 50th year as an actress, honored for her work with the National Repertory Theaters.

1965

MUSICAL
☆ *Fiddler on the Roof*. Music by Jerry Bock, lyrics by Sheldon Harnick, book by Joseph Stein. Produced by Harold Prince.

Golden Boy. Music by Charles Strouse, lyrics by Lee Adams, book by Clifford Odets and William Gibson. Produced by Hillard Elkins.

Half a Sixpence. Music and lyrics by David Heneker, book by Beverly Cross. Produced by Allen Hodgdon, Stevens Productions, and Harold Fielding.

Oh, What a Lovely War. Devised by Joan Littlewood for Theatre Workshop, Charles Chilton, and Members of the Cast. Produced by David Merrick and Gerry Raffles.

PLAY

Luv by Murray Schisgal. Produced by Claire Nichtern.

The Odd Couple by Neil Simon. Produced by Saint-Subber.

☆ *The Subject Was Roses* by Frank Gilroy. Produced by Edgar Lansbury.

Tiny Alice by Edward Albee. Produced by Theatre 1965, Richard Barr, and Clinton Wilder.

LEADING ACTOR (PLAY)

John Gielgud, *Tiny Alice*
☆ Walter Matthau, *The Odd Couple*
Donald Pleasence, *Poor Bitos*
Jason Robards, *Hughie*

LEADING ACTRESS (PLAY)

Marjorie Rhodes, *All in Good Time*
Bea Richards, *The Amen Corner*
Diana Sands, *The Owl and the Pussycat*
☆ Irene Worth, *Tiny Alice*

FEATURED ACTOR (PLAY)

☆ Jack Albertson, *The Subject Was Roses*
Murray Hamilton, *Absence of a Cello*
Martin Sheen, *The Subject Was Roses*
Clarence Williams III, *Slow Dance on the Killing Ground*

FEATURED ACTRESS (PLAY)

Rae Allen, *Traveller Without Language*
Alexandra Berlin, *All in Good Time*
Carolan Daniels, *Slow Dance on the Killing Ground*
☆ Alice Ghostley, *The Sign in Sidney Brustein's Window*

LEADING ACTOR (MUSICAL)

Sammy Davis, *Golden Boy*
☆ Zero Mostel, *Fiddler on the Roof*
Cyril Ritchard, *The Roar of the Greasepaint—The Smell of the Crowd*

Tommy Steele, *Half a Sixpence*

LEADING ACTRESS (MUSICAL)
Elizabeth Allen, *Do I Hear a Waltz?*
Nancy Dussault, *Bajour*
☆ Liza Minnelli, *Flora, the Red Menace*
Inga Swenson, *Baker Street*

FEATURED ACTOR (MUSICAL)
Jack Cassidy, *Fade Out—Fade In*
James Grout, *Half a Sixpence*
☆ Victor Spinetti, *Oh, What a Lovely War*
Jerry Orbach, *Guys and Dolls*

FEATURED ACTRESS (MUSICAL)
☆ Maria Karnilova, *Fiddler on the Roof*
Luba Lisa, *I Had a Ball*
Carrie Nye, *Half a Sixpence*
Barbara Windsor, *Oh, What a Lovely War*

AUTHOR (PLAY)
Edward Albee, *Tiny Alice*
Frank Gilroy, *The Subject Was Roses*
Murray Schisgal, *Luv*
☆ Neil Simon, *The Odd Couple*

PRODUCER (PLAY)
Hume Cronyn, Allen-Hogdon Inc., Stevens Productions Inc., and
 Bonfils- Seawell Enterprises, *Slow Dance on the Killing
 Ground*
☆ Claire Nichtern, *Luv*
Theatre 1965, Richard Barr, and Clinton Wilder, *Tiny Alice*
Robert Whitehead, *Tartuffe*

DIRECTOR (PLAY)
William Ball, *Tartuffe*
Ulu Grosbard, *The Subject Was Roses*
☆ Mike Nichols, *Luv* and *The Odd Couple*
Alan Schneider, *Tiny Alice*

AUTHOR (MUSICAL)
Jerome Coopersmith, *Baker Street*
Beverly Cross, *Half a Sixpence*
Sidney Michaels, *Ben Franklin in Paris*
☆ Joseph Stein, *Fiddler on the Roof*

PRODUCER (MUSICAL)
Allen-Hodgdon, Stevens Productions, and Harold Fielding, *Half a Sixpence*
Hillard Elkins, *Golden Boy*
David Merrick, *The Roar of the Greasepaint—The Smell of the Crowd*
☆ Harold Prince, *Fiddler on the Roof*

DIRECTOR (MUSICAL)
Joan Littlewood, *Oh, What a Lovely War*
Anthony Newley, *The Roar of the Greasepaint—The Smell of the Crowd*
☆ Jerome Robbins, *Fiddler on the Roof*
Gene Saks, *Half a Sixpence*

COMPOSER AND LYRICIST
☆ Jerry Bock and Sheldon Harnick, *Fiddler on the Roof*
Leslie Bricusse and Anthony Newley, *The Roar of the Greasepaint—The Smell of the Crowd*
David Heneker, *Half a Sixpence*
Richard Rodgers and Stephen Sondheim, *Do I Hear a Waltz?*

SCENIC DESIGNER
Boris Aronson, *Fiddler on the Roof* and *Incident at Vichy*
Sean Kenny, *The Roar of the Greasepaint—The Smell of the Crowd*
Beni Montresor, *Do I Hear a Waltz?*
☆ Oliver Smith, ☆ *Baker Street*, *Luv*, and *The Odd Couple*

COSTUME DESIGNER
Jane Greenwood, *Tartuffe*
Motley, *Baker Street*
Freddy Wittop, *The Roar of the Greasepaint—The Smell of the Crowd*
☆ Patricia Zipprodt, *Fiddler on the Roof*

CHOREOGRAPHER
Peter Gennaro, *Bajour*
Donald McKayle, *Golden Boy*
☆ Jerome Robbins, *Fiddler on the Roof*
Onna White, *Half a Sixpence*

SPECIAL AWARDS
☆ Gilbert Miller, for having produced 88 plays and musicals and for his perseverance which has helped to keep New York theatre alive.
☆ Oliver Smith

1966

MUSICAL

Mame. Book by Jerome Lawrence and Robert E. Lee, music and lyrics by Jerry Herman. Produced by Sylvia and Joseph Harris, Robert Fryer, and Lawrence Carr.

☆ *Man of La Mancha*. Book by Dale Wasserman, music by Mitch Leigh, lyrics by Joe Darion. Produced by Albert W. Selden and Hal James.

Skyscraper. Book by Peter Stone, music by James Van Heusen, lyrics by Sammy Cahn. Produced by Cy Feuer and Ernest M. Martin.

Sweet Charity. Book by Neil Simon, music by Cy Coleman, lyrics by Dorothy Fields. Produced by Sylvia and Joseph Harris, Robert Fryer, and Lawrence Carr.

PLAY

Inadmissible Evidence by John Osborne. Produced by the David Merrick Arts Foundation.

☆ *Marat / Sade* by Peter Weiss. English version by Geoffrey Skelton. Produced by the David Merrick Arts Foundation.

Philadelphia, Here I Come! by Brian Friel. Produced by the David Merrick Arts Foundation.

The Right Honourable Gentleman by Michael Dyne. Produced by Peter Cookson, Amy Lynn, and Walter Schwimmer.

LEADING ACTOR (PLAY)

Roland Culver, *Ivanov*
Donal Donnelly and Patrick Bedford, *Philadelphia, Here I Come!*
☆ Hal Holbrook, *Mark Twain Tonight!*
Nicol Williamson, *Inadmissible Evidence*

LEADING ACTRESS (PLAY)

Sheila Hancock, *Entertaining Mr. Sloane*
☆ Rosemary Harris, *The Lion in Winter*
Kate Reid, *Slapstick Tragedy*
Lee Remick, *Wait Until Dark*

FEATURED ACTOR (PLAY)

Burt Brinckerhoff, *Cactus Flower*
A. Larry Haines, *Generation*
Eamon Kelly, *Philadelphia, Here I Come!*
☆ Patrick Magee, *Marat / Sade*

FEATURED ACTRESS (PLAY)
☆ Zoe Caldwell, *Slapstick Tragedy*
Glenda Jackson, *Marat / Sade*
Mairin D. O'Sullivan, *Philadelphia, Here I Come!*
Brenda Vaccaro, *Cactus Flower*

LEADING ACTOR (MUSICAL)
Jack Cassidy, *Superman*
John Cullum, *On a Clear Day You Can See Forever*
☆ Richard Kiley, *Man of La Mancha*
Harry Secombe, *Pickwick*

LEADING ACTRESS (MUSICAL)
Barbara Harris, *On a Clear Day You Can See Forever*
Julie Harris, *Skyscraper*
☆ Angela Lansbury, *Mame*
Gwen Verdon, *Sweet Charity*

FEATURED ACTOR (MUSICAL)
Roy Castle, *Pickwick*
John McMartin, *Sweet Charity*
☆ Frankie Michaels, *Mame*
Michael O'Sullivan, *Superman*

FEATURED ACTRESS (MUSICAL)
☆ Beatrice Arthur, *Mame*
Helen Gallagher, *Sweet Charity*
Patricia Marand, *Superman*
Charlotte Rae, *Pickwick*

DIRECTOR (PLAY)
☆ Peter Brook, *Marat/Sade*
Hilton Edwards, *Philadelphia, Here I Come!*
Ellis Rabb, *You Can't Take It With You*
Noel Willman, *The Lion in Winter*

DIRECTOR (MUSICAL)
Cy Feuer, *Skyscraper*
Bob Fosse, *Sweet Charity*
☆ Albert Marre, *Man of La Mancha*
Gene Saks, *Mame*

COMPOSER AND LYRICIST
Cy Coleman and Dorothy Fields, *Sweet Charity*
Jerry Herman, *Mame*
☆ Mitch Leigh and Joe Darion, *Man of La Mancha*

Burton Lane and Alan Jay Lerner, *On a Clear Day You Can See Forever*

SCENIC DESIGNER
☆ Howard Bay, *Man of La Mancha*
William and Jean Eckart, *Mame*
David Hays, *Drat! The Cat!*
Robert Randolph, *Anya*, *Skyscraper*, and *Sweet Charity*

COSTUME DESIGNER
Loudon Sainthill, *The Right Honourable Gentleman*
Howard Bay and Patton Campbell, *Man of La Mancha*
Irene Sharaff, *Sweet Charity*
☆ Gunilla Palmstierna-Weiss, *Marat / Sade*

CHOREOGRAPHER
Jack Cole, *Man of La Mancha*
☆ Bob Fosse, *Sweet Charity*
Michael Kidd, *Skyscraper*
Onna White, *Mame*

SPECIAL AWARD
☆ Helen Menken (posthumous), for a lifetime of devotion and
dedicated service to the Broadway theatre.

1967

MUSICAL
☆ *Cabaret.* Music by John Kander, lyrics by Fred Ebb, book by
Joe Masteroff. Produced by Harold Prince in association
with Ruth Mitchell.
I Do! I Do! Music by Harvey Schmidt, book and lyrics by Tom
Jones. Produced by David Merrick.
The Apple Tree. Music by Jerry Bock, lyrics by Sheldon Harnick,
book by Sheldon Harnick and Jerry Bock. Produced by
Stuart Ostrow.
Walking Happy. Music by James Van Heusen, lyrics by Sammy
Cahn, book by Roger O. Hirson and Ketti Frings.
Produced by Cy Feuer and Ernest H. Martin.

PLAY
A Delicate Balance by Edward Albee. Produced by Theatre 1967,
Richard Barr, and Clinton Wilder.
Black Comedy by Peter Shaffer. Produced by Alexander H. Cohen.
☆ *The Homecoming* by Harold Pinter. Produced by Alexander H.
Cohen.

The *Killing of Sister George* by Frank Marcus. Produced by Helen
 Bonfils and Morton Gottlieb.

LEADING ACTOR (PLAY)
Hume Cronyn, A *Delicate Balance*
Donald Madden, *Black Comedy*
Donald Moffat, *Right You Are* and *The Wild Duck*
☆   Paul Rogers, *The Homecoming*

LEADING ACTRESS (PLAY)
Eileen Atkins, *The Killing of Sister George*
Vivian Merchant, *The Homecoming*
Rosemary Murphy, A *Delicate Balance*
☆   Beryl Reid, *The Killing of Sister George*

FEATURED ACTOR (PLAY)
Clayton Corzatte, *The School for Scandal*
Stephen Elliott, *Marat / Sade*
☆   Ian Holm, *The Homecoming*
Sydney Walker, *The Wild Duck*

FEATURED ACTRESS (PLAY)
Camilla Ashland, *Black Comedy*
Brenda Forbes, *The Loves of Cass McGuire*
☆   Marian Seldes, A *Delicate Balance*
Maria Tucci, *The Rose Tattoo*

LEADING ACTOR (MUSICAL)
Alan Alda, *The Apple Tree*
Jack Gilford, *Cabaret*
☆   Robert Preston, *I Do! I Do!*
Norman Wisdom, *Walking Happy*

LEADING ACTRESS (MUSICAL)
☆   Barbara Harris, *The Apple Tree*
Lotte Lenya, *Cabaret*
Mary Martin, *I Do! I Do!*
Louise Troy, *Walking Happy*

FEATURED ACTOR (MUSICAL)
Leon Bibb, A *Hand is on the Gate*
Gordon Dilworth, *Walking Happy*
☆   Joel Grey, *Cabaret*
Edward Winter, *Cabaret*

FEATURED ACTRESS (MUSICAL)
☆   Peg Murray, *Cabaret*

Leland Palmer, A *Joyful Noise*
Josephine Premice, A *Hand Is on the Gate*
Susan Watson, A *Joyful Noise*

DIRECTOR (PLAY)
John Dexter, *Black Comedy*
Donald Driver, *Marat / Sade*
☆ Peter Hall, *The Homecoming*
Alan Schneider, A *Delicate Balance*

DIRECTOR (MUSICAL)
Gower Champion, *I Do! I Do!*
Mike Nichols, *The Apple Tree*
Jack Sydow, *Annie Get Your Gun*
☆ Harold Prince, *Cabaret*

COMPOSER AND LYRICIST
Jerry Bock and Sheldon Harnick, *The Apple Tree*
Sammy Cahn and James Van Heusen, *Walking Happy*
Tom Jones and Harvey Schmidt, *I Do! I Do!*
☆ John Kander and Fred Ebb, *Cabaret*

SCENIC DESIGNER
☆ Boris Aronson, *Cabaret*
John Bury, *The Homecoming*
Oliver Smith, *I Do! I Do!*
Alan Tagg, *Black Comedy*

CHOREOGRAPHER
Michael Bennett, A *Joyful Noise*
Danny Daniels, *Walking Happy* and *Annie Get Your Gun*
☆ Ron Field, *Cabaret*
Lee Theodore, *The Apple Tree*

COSTUME DESIGNER
Nancy Potts, *The Wild Duck* and *The School for Scandal*
Tony Walton, *The Apple Tree*
Freddy Wittop, *I Do! I Do!*
☆ Patricia Zipprodt, *Cabaret*

1968

MUSICAL
☆ *Hallelujah, Baby!* Music by Jule Styne, lyrics by Betty Comden
and Adolph Green, book by Arthur Laurents. Produced by

Albert Selden, Hal James, Jane C. Nusbaum, and Harry Rigby.

The Happy Time. Music by John Kander, lyrics by Fred Ebb, book by N. Richard Nash. Produced by David Merrick.

How Now, Dow Jones. Music by Elmer Bernstein, lyrics by Carolyn Leigh, book by Max Shulman. Produced by David Merrick.

Illya, Darling. Music by Manos Hadjidakis, lyrics by Joe Darion, book by Jules Dassin. Produced by Kermit Bloomgarden.

PLAY

Joe Egg by Peter Nichols. Produced by Joseph Cates and Henry Fownes.

Plaza Suite by Neil Simon. Produced by Saint-Subber.

☆ *Rosencrantz and Guildenstern Are Dead* by Tom Stoppard. Produced by The David Merrick Arts Foundation.

The Price by Arthur Miller. Produced by Robert Whitehead.

LEADING ACTOR (PLAY)

☆ Martin Balsam, *You Know I Can't Hear You When the Water's Running*
Albert Finney, *Joe Egg*
Milo O'Shea, *Staircase*
Alan Webb, *I Never Sang for My Father*

LEADING ACTRESS (PLAY)

☆ Zoe Caldwell, *The Prime of Miss Jean Brodie*
Colleen Dewhurst, *More Stately Mansions*
Maureen Stapleton, *Plaza Suite*
Dorothy Tutin, *Portrait of a Queen*

FEATURED ACTOR (PLAY)

Paul Hecht, *Rosencrantz and Guildenstern Are Dead*
Brian Murray, *Rosencrantz and Guildenstern Are Dead*
☆ James Patterson, *The Birthday Party*
John Wood, *Rosencrantz and Guildenstern Are Dead*

FEATURED ACTRESS (PLAY)

Pert Kelton, *Spofford*
☆ Zena Walker, *Joe Egg*
Ruth White, *The Birthday Party*
Eleanor Wilson, *Weekend*

LEADING ACTOR (MUSICAL)

☆ Robert Goulet, *The Happy Time*
Robert Hooks, *Hallelujah, Baby!*
Anthony Roberts, *How Now, Dow Jones*

David Wayne, T*he Happy Time*

LEADING ACTRESS (MUSICAL)
Melinda Mercouri, *Illya Darling*
☆ Patricia Routledge, *Darling of the Day*
☆ Leslie Uggams, *Hallelujah, Baby!*
Brenda Vaccaro, *How Now, Dow Jones*

FEATURED ACTOR (MUSICAL)
Scott Jacoby, *Golden Rainbow*
Nikos Kourkoulous, *Illya Darling*
Mike Rupert, T*he Happy Time*
☆ Hiram Sherman, *How Now, Dow Jones*

FEATURED ACTRESS (MUSICAL)
Geula Gill, T*he Grand Music Hall of Israel*
Julie Gregg, T*he Happy Time*
☆ Lillian Hayman, *Hallelujah, Baby!*
Alice Playten, *Henry, Sweet Henry*

PRODUCER (PLAY)
☆ David Merrick Arts Foundation, *Rosencrantz and Guildenstern Are Dead*

DIRECTOR (PLAY)
Michael Blakemore, *Joe Egg*
Derek Goldby, *Rosencrantz and Guildenstern* Are Dead
☆ Mike Nichols, *Plaza Suite*
Alan Schneider, *You Know* I *Can't Hear You When the Water's Running*

PRODUCER (MUSICAL)
☆ Albert Selden, Hal James, Jane C. Nusbaum, and Harry Rigby, *Hallelujah, Baby!*

DIRECTOR (MUSICAL)
George Abbott, *How Now, Dow Jones*
☆ Gower Champion, T*he Happy Time*
Jules Dassin, *Illya, Darling*
Burt Shevelove, *Hallelujah, Baby!*

COMPOSER AND LYRICIST
Elmer Bernstein and Carolyn Leigh, *How Now, Dow Jones*
Manos Hadjidakis and Joe Darion, *Illya, Darling*
John Kander and Fred Ebb, T*he Happy Time*
☆ Jule Styne, Betty Comden, and Adolph Green, *Hallelujah, Baby!*

SCENIC DESIGNER
Boris Aronson, *The Price*
☆ Desmond Heeley, *Rosencrantz and Guildenstern Are Dead*
Robert Randolph, *Golden Rainbow*
Peter Wexler, *The Happy Time*

COSTUME DESIGNER
Jane Greenwood, *More Stately Mansions*
☆ Desmond Heeley, *Rosencrantz and Guildenstern Are Dead*
Irene Sharaff, *Hallelujah, Baby!*
Freddy Wittop, *The Happy Time*

CHOREOGRAPHER
Michael Bennett, *Henry, Sweet Henry*
Kevin Carlisle, *Hallelujah, Baby!*
☆ Gower Champion, *The Happy Time*
Onna White, *Illya Darling*

SPECIAL AWARDS
☆ Audrey Hepburn
☆ Carol Channing
☆ Pearl Bailey
☆ David Merrick
☆ Maurice Chevalier
☆ APA-Phoenix Theatre
☆ Marlene Dietrich

1969

MUSICAL
Hair. Music by Galt McDermot, lyrics by James Rado, book by Gerome Ragni and James Rado. Produced by Michael Butler.
Promises, Promises. Music and lyrics by Burt Bacharach, book by Neil Simon. Produced by David Merrick.
☆ *1776.* Music and lyrics by Sherman Edwards, book by Peter Stone. Produced by Stuart Ostrow.
Zorba. Music by John Kander, lyrics by Fred Ebb, book by Joseph Stein. Produced by Harold Prince.

PLAY
☆ *The Great White Hope* by Howard Sackler. Produced by Herman Levin.

Hadrian VII by Peter Luke. Produced by Lester Osterman
Productions, Bill Freedman, and Charles Kasher.
Lovers by Brian Friel. Produced by Helen Bonfils and Morton
Gottlieb.
The Man in the Glass Booth by Robert Shaw. Produced by
Glasshouse Productions and Peter Bridge, Ivor David
Balding & Associates Ltd., and Edward M. Meyers with
Leslie Ogden.

LEADING ACTOR (PLAY)
Art Carney, *Lovers*
☆ James Earl Jones, *The Great White Hope*
Alec McCowen, *Hadrian VII*
Donald Pleasence, *The Man in the Glass Booth*

LEADING ACTRESS (PLAY)
☆ Julie Harris, *Forty Carats*
Estelle Parsons, *Seven Descents of Myrtle*
Charlotte Rae, *Morning, Noon and Night*
Brenda Vaccaro, *The Goodbye People*

FEATURED ACTOR (PLAY)
☆ Al Pacino, *Does a Tiger Wear a Necktie?*
Richard Castellano, *Lovers and Other Strangers*
Anthony Roberts, *Play It Again, Sam*
Louis Zorich, *Hadrian VII*

FEATURED ACTRESS (PLAY)
☆ Jane Alexander, *The Great White Hope*
Diane Keaton, *Play It Again, Sam*
Lauren Jones, *Does a Tiger Wear a Necktie?*
Anna Manahan, *Lovers*

LEADING ACTOR (MUSICAL)
Herschel Bernardi, *Zorba*
Jack Cassidy, *Maggie Flynn*
Joel Grey, *George M!*
☆ Jerry Orbach, *Promises, Promises*

LEADING ACTRESS (MUSICAL)
Maria Karnilova, *Zorba*
☆ Angela Lansbury, *Dear World*
Dorothy Loudon, *The Fig Leaves Are Falling*
Jill O'Hara, *Promises, Promises*

FEATURED ACTOR (MUSICAL)
A. Larry Haines, *Promises, Promises*

☆ Ronald Holgate, 1776
Edward Winter, *Promises, Promises*

FEATURED ACTRESS (MUSICAL)

Sandy Duncan, *Canterbury Tales*
☆ Marian Mercer, *Promises, Promises*
Lorraine Serabian, *Zorba*
Virginia Vestoff, 1776

DIRECTOR (PLAY)

☆ Peter Dews, *Hadrian VII*
Joseph Hardy, *Play It Again, Sam*
Harold Pinter, *The Man in the Glass Booth*
Michael A. Schultz, *Does a Tiger Wear a Necktie?*

DIRECTOR (MUSICAL)

☆ Peter Hunt, 1776
Robert Moore, *Promises, Promises*
Tom O' Horgan, *Hair*
Harold Prince, *Zorba*

SCENIC DESIGNER

☆ Boris Aronson, *Zorba*
Derek Cousins, *Canterbury Tales*
Jo Mielziner, 1776
Oliver Smith, *Dear World*

COSTUME DESIGNER

Michael Annals, *Morning, Noon and Night*
Robert Fletcher, *Hadrian VII*
☆ Louden Sainthill, *Canterbury Tales*
Patricia Zipprodt, *Zorba*

CHOREOGRAPHER

Sammy Bayes, *Canterbury Tales*
Ronald Field, *Zorba*
☆ Joe Layton, *George M!*
Michael Bennett, *Promises, Promises*

SPECIAL AWARDS

☆ The National Theatre Company of Great Britain
☆ The Negro Ensemble Company
☆ Rex Harrison
☆ Leonard Bernstein
☆ Carol Burnett

The 1970s

"**L**ighting *design as an art and craft in the theatre is one that receives little notice. And rightly so, because light itself is invisible and only enables you to see objects and humans that the light falls upon. For the majority of theatrical productions lighting is an unseen tool that guides the audience's eyes and aids in creating a mood and atmosphere. Thus when lighting is very good it is hardly noticed, and only on a subconscious level can you connect the quality of the lighting with the overall enjoyment and appreciation of the play. Thus, for many years I have taken pride in the fact that when I had done my best work no one might notice and thus I could rationalize why I had never received any awards for my work.*

"Now that I have won a Tony Award I must work even harder to make my work unseen and keep it a secret so that more people can enjoy the theatre."

Jules Fisher
Lighting Designer, *Pippin*
Lighting Designer, *Ulysses in Nighttown*
Lighting Design, *Dancin'*
Lighting Designer, *Grand Hotel, The Musical*
Lighting Designer, *The Will Rogers Follies*
Lighting Designer, *Jelly's Last Jam*
Lighting Designer, *Bring in 'Da Noise, Bring in 'Da Funk*

JOHN KANDER, BARBRA STREISAND, AND FRED EBB

1970

MUSICAL

☆ *Applause*. Music by Charles Strouse, lyrics by Lee Adams, book by Betty Comden and Adolph Green. Produced by Joseph Kipness and Lawrence Kasha.

Coco. Music by André Previn, book and lyrics by Alan Jay Lerner. Produced by Frederick Brisson.

Purlie. Music by Gary Geld, lyrics by Peter Udell, book by Ossie Davis, Philip Rose, and Peter Udell. Produced by Philip Rose.

PLAY

☆ *Borstal Boy* by Frank McMahon. Produced by Michael McAloney and Burton C. Kaiser.

Child's Play by Robert Marasco. Produced by David Merrick.

Indians by Arthur Kopit. Produced by Lyn Austin, Oliver Smith, Joel Schenker, and Roger L. Stevens.

Last of the Red Hot Lovers by Neil Simon. Produced by Saint-Subber.

LEADING ACTOR (PLAY)

James Coco, *Last of the Red Hot Lovers*
Frank Grimes, *Borstal Boy*
Stacy Keach, *Indians*
☆ Fritz Weaver, *Child's Play*

LEADING ACTRESS (PLAY)

Geraldine Brooks, *Brightower*
☆ Tammy Grimes, *Private Lives*
Helen Hayes, *Harvey* (Revival)

FEATURED ACTOR (PLAY)

Joseph Bova, *The Chinese and Dr. Fish*
☆ Ken Howard, *Child's Play*
Dennis King, *A Patriot for Me*

FEATURED ACTRESS (PLAY)

☆ Blythe Danner, *Butterflies Are Free*
Alice Drummond, *The Chinese and Dr. Fish*
Eileen Heckart, *Butterflies Are Free*
Linda Lavin, *Last of the Red Hot Lovers*

LEADING ACTOR (MUSICAL)

Len Cariou, *Applause*
☆ Cleavon Little, *Purlie*
Robert Weede, *Cry for Us All*

LEADING ACTRESS (MUSICAL)
☆ Lauren Bacall, *Applause*
Katharine Hepburn, *Coco*
Dilys Watling, *Georgy*

FEATURED ACTOR (MUSICAL)
☆ René Auberjonois, *Coco*
Brandon Maggart, *Applause*
George Rose, *Coco*

FEATURED ACTRESS (MUSICAL)
Bonnie Franklin, *Applause*
Penny Fuller, *Applause*
Melissa Hart, *Georgy*
☆ Melba Moore, *Purlie*

DIRECTOR (PLAY)
☆ Joseph Hardy, *Child's Play*
Milton Katselas, *Butterflies Are Free*
Tomas MacAnna, *Borstal Boy*
Robert Moore, *Last of the Red Hot Lovers*

DIRECTOR (MUSICAL)
Michael Benthall, *Coco*
☆ Ron Field, *Applause*
Philip Rose, *Purlie*

SCENIC DESIGNER
Howard Bay, *Cry for Us All*
Ming Cho Lee, *Billy*
☆ Jo Mielziner, *Child's Play*
Robert Randolph, *Applause*

COSTUME DESIGNER
Ray Aghayan, *Applause*
☆ Cecil Beaton, *Coco*
W. Robert Lavine, *Jimmy*
Freddy Wittop, *A Patriot for Me*

LIGHTING DESIGNER
☆ Jo Mielziner, *Child's Play*
Tharon Musser, *Applause*
Thomas Skelton, *Indians*

CHOREOGRAPHER
Michael Bennett, *Coco*
Grover Dale, *Billy*

☆ Ron Field, *Applause*
Louis Johnson, *Purlie*

SPECIAL AWARDS

☆ Noel Coward, for his multiple and immortal contributions to the theatre.
☆ Alfred Lunt and Lynn Fontanne
☆ New York Shakespeare Festival, for pioneering efforts on behalf of new plays.
☆ Barbra Streisand

1971

MUSICAL

☆ *Company.* Produced by Harold Prince.
The Me Nobody Knows. Produced by Jeff Britton.
The Rothschilds. Produced by Lester Osterman and Hillard Elkins.

PLAY

Home by David Storey. Produced by Alexander H. Cohen.
☆ *Sleuth* by Anthony Shaffer. Produced by Helen Bonfils, Morton Gottlieb, and Michael White.
Story Theatre by Paul Sills. Produced by Zev Bufman.
The Philanthropist by Christopher Hampton. Produced by David Merrick and Byron Goldman.

LEADING ACTOR (PLAY)

☆ Brian Bedford, *The School for Wives*
John Gielgud, *Home*
Alec McCowen, *The Philanthropist*
Ralph Richardson, *Home*

LEADING ACTRESS (PLAY)

Estelle Parsons, *And Miss Reardon Drinks a Little*
Diana Rigg, *Abelard and Heloise*
Marian Seldes, *Father's Day*
☆ Maureen Stapleton, *The Gingerbread Lady*

FEATURED ACTOR (PLAY)

Ronald Radd, *Abelard and Heloise*
Donald Pickering, *Conduct Unbecoming*
☆ Paul Sand, *Story Theatre*
Ed Zimmermann, *The Philanthropist*

FEATURED ACTRESS (PLAY)
☆ Rae Allen, *And Miss Reardon Drinks a Little*
Lili Darvas, *Les Blancs*
Joan Van Ark, *The School for Wives*
Mona Washbourne, *Home*

LEADING ACTOR (MUSICAL)
David Burns, *Lovely Ladies, Kind Gentlemen*
Larry Kert, *Company*
☆ Hal Linden, *The Rothschilds*
Bobby Van, *No, No, Nanette*

LEADING ACTRESS (MUSICAL)
Susan Browning, *Company*
Sandy Duncan, *The Boyfriend*
☆ Helen Gallagher, *No, No, Nanette*
Elaine Stritch, *Company*

FEATURED ACTOR (MUSICAL)
☆ Keene Curtis, *The Rothschilds*
Charles Kimbrough, *Company*
Walter Willison, *Two By Two*

FEATURED ACTRESS (MUSICAL)
Barbara Barrie, *Company*
☆ Patsy Kelly, *No, No, Nanette*
Pamela Myers, *Company*

PRODUCER (PLAY)
Alexander H. Cohen, *Home*
David Merrick, *The Philanthropist*
☆ Helen Bonfils, Morton Gottlieb, and Michael White, *Sleuth*
Zev Bufman, *Story Theatre*

DIRECTOR (PLAY)
Lindsay Anderson, *Home*
☆ Peter Brook, *A Midsummer Night's Dream*
Stephen Porter, *The School for Wives*
Clifford Williams, *Sleuth*

PRODUCER (MUSICAL)
Jeff Britton, *The Me Nobody Knows*
Hillard Elkins and Lester Osterman, *The Rothschilds*
☆ Harold Prince, *Company*

DIRECTOR (MUSICAL)
Michael Kidd, *The Rothschilds*

Robert H. Livingston, *The Me Nobody Knows*
☆ Harold Prince, *Company*
Burt Shevelove, *No, No, Nanette*

BOOK (MUSICAL)
☆ George Furth, *Company*
Robert H. Livingston and Herb Schapiro, *The Me Nobody Knows*
Sherman Yellen, *The Rothschilds*

LYRICS
Sheldon Harnick, *The Rothschilds*
Will Holt, *The Me Nobody Knows*
☆ Stephen Sondheim, *Company*

SCORE
Jerry Bock, *The Rothschilds*
Gary William Friedman, *The Me Nobody Knows*
☆ Stephen Sondheim, *Company*

SCENIC DESIGNER
☆ Boris Aronson, *Company*
John Bury, *The Rothschilds*
Sally Jacobs, *A Midsummer Night's Dream*
Jo Mielziner, *Father's Day*

COSTUME DESIGNER
☆ Raoul Pène du Bois, *No, No, Nanette*
Jane Greenwood, *Hay Fever*
Jane Greenwood, *Les Blancs*
Freddy Wittop, *Lovely Ladies, Kind Gentlemen*

LIGHTING DESIGNER
Robert Ornbo, *Company*
☆ H.R. Poindexter, *Story Theatre*
William Ritman, *Sleuth*

CHOREOGRAPHER
Michael Bennett, *Company*
Michael Kidd, *The Rothschilds*
☆ Donald Saddler, *No, No, Nanette*

SPECIAL AWARDS
☆ Elliot Norton, drama critic, for distinguished theatrical commentary.
☆ Ingram Ash, for decades of devoted service to the theatre as president of Blaine-Thompson Advertising.
☆ Playbill, for chronicling Broadway through the years.

☆ Roger L. Stevens for helping to focus government attention on the arts.

1972

MUSICAL
Ain't Supposed to Die a Natural Death. Produced by Eugene V. Wolsk, Charles Blackwell, Emanuel Azenberg, and Robert Malina.
Follies. Produced by Harold Prince.
☆ *Two Gentlemen of Verona.* Produced by New York Shakespeare Festival—Joseph Papp.
Grease. Produced by Kenneth Waissman and Maxine Fox.

PLAY
Old Times by Harold Pinter. Produced by Roger L. Stevens.
The Prisoner of Second Avenue by Neil Simon. Produced by Saint-Subber.
☆ *Sticks and Bones* by David Rabe. Produced by New York Shakespeare Festival—Joseph Papp.
Vivat! Vivat Regina! by Robert Bolt. Produced by David Merrick and Arthur Cantor.

LEADING ACTOR (PLAY)
Tom Aldredge, *Sticks and Bones*
Donald Pleasence, *Wise Child*
☆ Cliff Gorman, *Lenny*
Jason Robards, *The Country Girl*

LEADING ACTRESS (PLAY)
Eileen Atkins, *Vivat! Vivat Regina!*
Colleen Dewhurst, *All Over*
Rosemary Harris, *Old Times*
☆ Sada Thompson, *Twigs*

FEATURED ACTOR (PLAY)
☆ Vincent Gardenia, *The Prisoner of Second Avenue*
Douglas Rain, *Vivat! Vivat Regina!*
Lee Richardson, *Vivat! Vivat Regina!*
Joe Silver, *Lenny*

FEATURED ACTRESS (PLAY)
Cara Duff-MacCormick, *Moonchildren*
Mercedes McCambridge, *The Love Suicide at Schofield Barracks*
Frances Sternhagen, *The Sign in Sidney Brustein's Window*

☆   Elizabeth Wilson, *Sticks and Bones*

LEADING ACTOR (MUSICAL)
Clifton Davis, *Two Gentlemen of Verona*
Barry Bostwick, *Grease*
Raul Julia, *Two Gentlemen of Verona*
☆   Phil Silvers, *A Funny Thing Happened on the Way to the Forum*

LEADING ACTRESS (MUSICAL)
Jonelle Allen, *Two Gentlemen of Verona*
Dorothy Collins, *Follies*
Mildred Natwick, *70, Girls, 70*
☆   Alexis Smith, *Follies*

FEATURED ACTOR (MUSICAL)
☆   Larry Blyden, *A Funny Thing Happened on the Way to the Forum*
Timothy Myers, *Grease*
Gene Nelson, *Follies*
Ben Vereen, *Jesus Christ Superstar*

FEATURED ACTRESS (MUSICAL)
Adrienne Barbeau, *Grease*
☆   Linda Hopkins, *Inner City*
Bernadette Peters, *On the Town*
Beatrice Wind, *Ain't Supposed to Die a Natural Death*

DIRECTOR (PLAY)
Jeff Bleckner, *Sticks and Bones*
Gordon Davidson, *The Trial of the Catonsville Nine*
Peter Hall, *Old Times*
☆   Mike Nichols, *The Prisoner of Second Avenue*

DIRECTOR (MUSICAL)
Gilbert Moses, *Ain't Supposed to Die a Natural Death*
☆   Harold Prince and Michael Bennett, *Follies*
Mel Shapiro, *Two Gentlemen of Verona*
Burt Shevelove, *A Funny Thing Happened on the Way to the Forum*

BOOK (MUSICAL)
Ain't Supposed to Die a Natural Death by Melvin Van Peeples
Follies by James Goldman
Grease by Jim Jacobs and Warren Casey
☆   *Two Gentlemen of Verona* by John Guare and Mel Shapiro

SCORE
Ain't Supposed to Die a Natural Death. Music and lyrics by Melvin Van Peeples.
☆ Follies. Music and lyrics by Stephen Sondheim.
Jesus Christ Superstar. Music by Andrew Lloyd Webber, lyrics by Tim Rice.
Two Gentlemen of Verona. Music by Galt MacDermot, lyrics by John Guare.

SCENIC DESIGNER
☆ Boris Aronson, Follies
John Bury, Old Times
Kert Lundell, Ain't Supposed to Die a Natural Death
Robin Wagner, Jesus Christ Superstar

COSTUME DESIGNER
Theoni V. Aldredge, Two Gentlemen of Verona
Randy Barcelo, Jesus Christ Superstar
☆ Florence Klotz, Follies
Carrie F. Robbins, Grease

LIGHTING DESIGNER
Martin Aronstein, Ain't Supposed to Die a Natural Death
John Bury, Old Times
Jules Fisher, Jesus Christ Superstar
☆ Tharon Musser, Follies

CHOREOGRAPHER
☆ Michael Bennett, Follies
Patricia Birch, Grease
Jean Erdman, Two Gentlemen of Verona

SPECIAL AWARDS
☆ The Theatre Guild—American Theatre Society, for its many years of service to audiences for touring shows.
☆ Fiddler on the Roof, on becoming the longest-running musical in Broadway history. Presented to Harold S. Prince.
☆ Ethel Merman
☆ Richard Rodgers

1973

MUSICAL
☆ A Little Night Music. Produced by Harold Prince.

Photo: Anita and Steve Shevett

JULIE HARRIS

Don't Bother Me, I Can't Cope. Produced by Edward Padula and Arch Lustberg.
Pippin. Produced by Stuart Ostrow.
Sugar. Produced by David Merrick.

PLAY

Butley by Simon Gray. Produced by Lester Osterman and Richard Horner.
☆   *That Championship Season* by Jason Miller. Produced by the New York Shakespeare Festival—Joseph Papp.

The Changing Room by David Storey. Produced by Charles Bowden, Lee Reynolds, and Isobel Robins.

The Sunshine Boys by Neil Simon. Produced by Emanuel Azenberg and Eugene V. Wolsk.

LEADING ACTOR (PLAY)
Jack Albertson, The Sunshine Boys
☆ Alan Bates, Butley
Wilfrid Hyde White, The Jockey Club Stakes
Paul Sorvino, That Championship Season

LEADING ACTRESS (PLAY)
Jane Alexander, 6 Rms Riv Vu
Colleen Dewhurst, Mourning Becomes Electra
☆ Julie Harris, The Last of Mrs. Lincoln
Kathleen Widdoes, Much Ado About Nothing

FEATURED ACTOR (PLAY)
Barnard Hughes, Much Ado About Nothing
☆ John Lithgow, The Changing Room
John McMartin, Don Juan
Hayward Morse, Butley

FEATURED ACTRESS (PLAY)
Maya Angelou, Look Away
☆ Leora Dana, The Last of Mrs. Lincoln
Katherine Helmond, The Great God Brown
Penelope Windust, Elizabeth I

LEADING ACTOR (MUSICAL)
Len Cariou, A Little Night Music
Robert Morse, Sugar
Brock Peters, Lost in the Stars
☆ Ben Vereen, Pippin

LEADING ACTRESS (MUSICAL)
☆ Glynis Johns, A Little Night Music
Leland Palmer, Pippin
Debbie Reynolds, Irene
Marcia Rodd, Shelter

FEATURED ACTOR (MUSICAL)
Laurence Guittard, A Little Night Music
☆ George S. Irving, Irene
Avon Long, Don't Play Us Cheap
Gilbert Price, Lost in the Stars

FEATURED ACTRESS (MUSICAL)
☆ Patricia Elliot, A *Little Night Music*
Hermione Gingold, A *Little Night Music*
Patsy Kelly, *Irene*
Irene Ryan, *Pippin*

DIRECTOR (PLAY)
☆ A.J. Antoon, *That Championship Season*
A.J. Antoon, *Much Ado About Nothing*
Alan Arkin, *The Sunshine Boys*
Michael Rudman, *The Changing Room*

DIRECTOR (MUSICAL)
Vinnette Carroll, *Don't Bother Me, I Can't Cope*
Gower Champion, *Sugar*
☆ Bob Fosse, *Pippin*
Harold Prince, A *Little Night Music*

BOOK (MUSICAL)
Don't Bother Me, I Can't Cope by Micki Grant
Don't Play Us Cheap by Melvin Van Peeples
☆ A *Little Night Music* by Hugh Wheeler
Pippin by Roger O. Hirson

SCORE
Don't Bother Me, I Can't Cope. Music and lyrics by Micki Grant.
☆ A *Little Night Music.* Music and lyrics by Stephen Sondheim.
Much Ado About Nothing. Music by Peter Link.
Pippin. Music and lyrics by Stephen Schwartz.

SCENIC DESIGNER
Boris Aronson, A *Little Night Music*
David Jenkins, *The Changing Room*
Santo Loquasto, *That Championship Season*
☆ Tony Walton, *Pippin*

COSTUME DESIGNER
Theoni V. Aldredge, *Much Ado About Nothing*
☆ Florence Klotz, A *Little Night Music*
Miles White, *Tricks*
Patricia Zipprodt, *Pippin*

LIGHTING DESIGNER
Martin Aronstein, *Much Ado About Nothing*
Ian Calderon, *That Championship Season*
☆ Jules Fisher, *Pippin*

Tharon Musser, A *Little Night Music*

CHOREOGRAPHER
Gower Champion, *Sugar*
☆ Bob Fosse, *Pippin*
Peter Gennaro, *Irene*
Donald Saddler, *Much Ado About Nothing*

SPECIAL AWARDS
☆ John Lindsay, Mayor of New York City
☆ Actors' Fund of America
☆ Shubert Organization

1974

MUSICAL
Over Here! Produced by Kenneth Waissman and Maxine Fox.
☆ *Raisin.* Produced by Robert Nemiroff.
Seesaw. Produced by Joseph Kipness, Lawrence Kasha, James
  Nederlander, George M. Steinbrenner III, and Lorin E.
  Price.

PLAY
Boom Boom Room by David Rabe. Produced by Joseph Papp.
The Au Pair Man by Hugh Leonard. Produced by Joseph Papp.
☆ *The River Niger* by Joseph A. Walker. Produced by Negro
  Ensemble Co., Inc.
Ulysses in Nighttown by Marjorie Barkentin. Produced by Alexander
  H. Cohen and Bernard Delfont.

LEADING ACTOR (PLAY)
☆ Michael Moriarty, *Find Your Way Home*
Zero Mostel, *Ulysses in Nighttown*
Jason Robards, *A Moon for the Misbegotten*
George C. Scott, *Uncle Vanya*
Nicol Williamson, *Uncle Vanya*

LEADING ACTRESS (PLAY)
Jane Alexander, *Find Your Way Home*
☆ Colleen Dewhurst, *A Moon for the Misbegotten*
Julie Harris, *The Au Pair Man*
Madeline Kahn, *Boom Boom Room*
Rachel Roberts, performances with the *New Phoenix Repertory
  Company*

FEATURED ACTOR (PLAY)
René Auberjonois, *The Good Doctor*
☆ Ed Flanders, *A Moon for the Misbegotten*
Douglas Turner Ward, *The River Niger*
Dick Anthony Williams, *What the Wine-Sellers Buy*

FEATURED ACTRESS (PLAY)
Regina Baff, *Veronica's Room*
Fionnula Flanagan, *Ulysses in Nighttown*
Charlotte Moore, *Chemin de Fer*
Roxie Roker, *The River Niger*
☆ Frances Sternhagen, *The Good Doctor*

LEADING ACTOR (MUSICAL)
Alfred Drake, *Gigi*
Joe Morton, *Raisin*
☆ Christopher Plummer, *Cyrano*
Lewis J. Stadlen, *Candide*

LEADING ACTRESS (MUSICAL)
☆ Virginia Capers, *Raisin*
Carol Channing, *Lorelei*
Michele Lee, *Seesaw*

FEATURED ACTOR (MUSICAL)
Mark Baker, *Candide*
Ralph Carter, *Raisin*
☆ Tommy Tune, *Seesaw*

FEATURED ACTRESS (MUSICAL)
Leigh Berry, *Cyrano*
Maureen Brennan, *Candide*
June Gable, *Candide*
Ernestine Jackson, *Raisin*
☆ Janie Sell, *Over Here!*

DIRECTOR (PLAY)
Burgess Meredith, *Ulysses in Nighttown*
Mike Nichols, *Uncle Vanya*
Stephen Porter, *Chemin de Fer*
☆ José Quintero, *A Moon for the Misbegotten*
Edwin Sherin, *Find Your Way Home*

DIRECTOR (MUSICAL)
Michael Bennett, *Seesaw*

Donald McKayle, *Raisin*
Tom Moore, *Over Here!*
☆   Harold Prince, *Candide*

BOOK (MUSICAL)
☆   *Candide* by Hugh Wheeler
Raisin by Robert Nemiroff and Charlotte Zaltzberg
Seesaw by Michael Bennett

SCORE
☆   *Gigi*. Music by Frederick Loewe, lyrics by Alan Jay Lerner.
The Good Doctor. Music by Peter Link, lyrics by Neil Simon.
Raisin. Music by Judd Woldin, lyrics by Robert Brittan.
Seesaw. Music by Cy Coleman, lyrics by Dorothy Fields.

SCENIC DESIGNER
John Conklin, *The Au Pair Man*
☆   Franne and Eugene Lee, *Candide*
Santo Loquasto, *What the Wine-Sellers Buy*
Oliver Smith, *Gigi*
Ed Wittstein, *Ulysses in Nighttown*

COSTUME DESIGNER
Theoni V. Aldredge, *The Au Pair Man*
Finlay James, *Crown Matrimonial*
☆   Franne Lee, *Candide*
Oliver Messel, *Gigi*
Carrie F. Robbins, *Over Here!*

LIGHTING DESIGNER
Martin Aronstein, *Boom Boom Room*
Ken Billington, *The Visit*
Ben Edwards, *A Moon for the Misbegotten*
☆   Jules Fisher, *Ulysses in Nighttown*
Tharon Musser, *The Good Doctor*

CHOREOGRAPHER
☆   Michael Bennett, *Seesaw*
Patricia Birch, *Over Here!*
Donald McKayle, *Raisin*

SPECIAL AWARDS
☆   Liza Minnelli, for adding lustre to the Broadway season.
☆   Bette Midler, for adding lustre to the Broadway season.
☆   Peter Cook and Dudley Moore, co-stars and authors of *Good
     Evening*.

☆ A *Moon for the Misbegotten*, an outstanding dramatic revival of an American classic, produced by Lester Osterman, Elliot Martin, and Richard Horner.

☆ *Candide*, an outstanding contribution to the artistic development of the musical theatre, produced by Chelsea Theatre Group, Harold Prince, and Ruth Mitchell.

☆ Actors' Equity Association

☆ Theatre Development Fund

☆ John F. Wharton, veteran theatrical attorney.

☆ Harold Friedlander, the industry's foremost printing expert.

1975

MUSICAL
Mack and Mabel. Produced by David Merrick.
The Lieutenant. Produced by Joseph Kutrzeba and Spofford Beadle.
Shenandoah. Produced by Philip Rose and Gloria and Louis K. Sher.
☆ *The Wiz*. Produced by Ken Harper.

PLAY
☆ *Equus* by Peter Shaffer. Produced by Kermit Bloomgarden and Doris Cole Abrahams.
Same Time, Next Year by Bernard Slade. Produced by Morton Gottlieb.
Seascape by Edward Albee. Produced by Richard Barr, Charles Woodward, and Clinton Wilder.
Short Eyes by Miguel Pinero. Produced by Joseph Papp, New York Shakespeare Festival.
Sizwe Banzi is Dead and The Island by Athol Fugard, John Kani, and Winston Ntshona. Produced by Hillard Elkins, Lester Osterman Productions, Bernard Delfront, and Michael White.
The National Health by Peter Nichols. Produced by Circle in the Square, Inc.

LEADING ACTOR (PLAY)
Jim Dale, *Scapino*
Peter Firth, *Equus*
Henry Fonda, *Clarence Darrow*
Ben Gazzara, *Hughie and Duet*
☆ John Kani and Winston Ntshona, *Sizwe Banzi is Dead and The Island*
John Wood, *Sherlock Holmes*

LEADING ACTRESS (PLAY)
Elizabeth Ashley, *Cat on a Hot Tin Roof*
☆ Ellen Burstyn, *Same Time, Next Year*
Diana Rigg, *The Misanthrope*
Maggie Smith, *Private Lives*
Liv Ullmann, *A Doll's House*

FEATURED ACTOR (PLAY)
Larry Blyden, *Absurd Person Singular*
Leonard Frey, *The National Health*
☆ Frank Langella, *Seascape*
Philip Locke, *Sherlock Holmes*
George Rose, *My Fat Friend*
Dick Anthony Williams, *Black Picture Show*

FEATURED ACTRESS (PLAY)
Linda Miller, *Black Picture Show*
☆ Rita Moreno, *The Ritz*
Geraldine Page, *Absurd Person Singular*
Carole Shelley, *Absurd Person Singular*
Elizabeth Spriggs, *London Assurance*
Frances Sternhagen, *Equus*

LEADING ACTOR (MUSICAL)
☆ John Cullum, *Shenandoah*
Joel Grey, *Goodtime Charley*
Raul Julia, *Where's Charley?*
Eddie Mekka, *The Lieutenant*
Robert Preston, *Mack and Mabel*

LEADING ACTRESS (MUSICAL)
Lola Falana, *Doctor Jazz*
☆ Angela Lansbury, *Gypsy*
Bernadette Peters, *Mack and Mabel*
Ann Reinking, *Goodtime Charley*

FEATURED ACTOR (MUSICAL)
Tom Aldredge, *Where's Charley?*
John Bottoms, *Dance with Me*
Doug Henning, *The Magic Show*
Gilbert Price, *The Night That Made America Famous*
☆ Ted Ross, *The Wiz*
Richard B. Schull, *Goodtime Charley*

FEATURED ACTRESS (MUSICAL)
☆ Dee Dee Bridgewater, *The Wiz*

Susan Browning, *Goodtime Charley*
Zan Charisse, *Gypsy*
Taina Elg, *Where's Charley?*
Kelly Garrett, *The Night That Made America Famous*
Donna Theodore, *Shenandoah*

DIRECTOR (PLAY)

Arvin Brown, *The National Health*
☆   John Dexter, *Equus*
Frank Dunlop, *Scapino*
Ronald Eyre, *London Assurance*
Athol Fugard, *Sizwe Banzi is Dead and The Island*
Gene Saks, *Same Time, Next Year*

DIRECTOR (MUSICAL)

Gower Champion, *Mack and Mabel*
Grover Dale, *The Magic Show*
☆   Geoffrey Holder, *The Wiz*
Arthur Laurents, *Gypsy*

BOOK (MUSICAL)

The Lieutenant by Gene Curty, Nitra Scharfman, and Chuck Strand
Mack and Mabel by Michael Stewart
☆   *Shenandoah* by James Lee Barrett, Peter Udell, and Philip Rose
The Wiz by William F. Brown

SCORE

Letter for Queen Victoria. Music and lyrics by Alan Lloyd.
The Lieutenant. Music and lyrics by Gene Curty, Nitra Scharfman, and Chuck Strand.
Shenandoah. Music by Gary Geld, lyrics by Peter Udell.
☆   *The Wiz.* Music and lyrics by Charlie Smalls.

SCENIC DESIGNER

Scott Johnson, *Dance With Me*
Tanya Moiseiwitsch, *The Misanthrope*
William Ritman, *God's Favorite*
Rouben Ter-Arutunian, *Goodtime Charley*
☆   Carl Toms, *Sherlock Holmes*
Robin Wagner, *Mack and Mabel*

COSTUME DESIGNER

Arthur Boccia, *Where's Charley?*
Raoul Pène du Bois, *Doctor Jazz*
☆   Geoffrey Holder, *The Wiz*
Willa Kim, *Goodtime Charley*

Tanya Moiseiwitsch, *The Misanthrope*
Patricia Zipprodt, *Mack and Mabel*

LIGHTING DESIGNER
Chip Monk, *The Rocky Horror Show*
Abe Feder, *Goodtime Charley*
☆   Neil Peter Jampolis, *Sherlock Holmes*
Andy Phillips, *Equus*
Thomas Skelton, *All God's Chillun Got Wings*
James Tilton, *Seascape*

CHOREOGRAPHER
Gower Champion, *Mack and Mabel*
☆   George Faison, *The Wiz*
Donald McKayle, *Doctor Jazz*
Margo Sappington, *Where's Charley?*
Robert Tucker, *Shenandoah*
Joel Zwick, *Dance with Me*

SPECIAL AWARD
☆   Neil Simon

1976

MUSICAL
☆   *A Chorus Line.* Produced by Joseph Papp, New York
     Shakespeare Festival.
Bubbling Brown Sugar. Produced by J. Lloyd Grant, Richard Bell,
     Robert M. Cooper, and Ashton Springer in association with
     Moe Septee, Inc.
Chicago. Produced by Robert Fryer and James Cresson.
Pacific Overtures. Produced by Harold Prince in association with
     Ruth Mitchell.

PLAY
The First Breeze of Summer by Leslie Lee. Produced by Negro
     Ensemble Co., Inc.
Knock Knock by Jules Feiffer. Produced by Harry Rigby and Terry
     Allen Kramer.
Lamppost Reunion by Louis LaRusso II. Produced by Joe Garofalo.
☆   *Travesties* by Tom Stoppard. Produced by David Merrick, Doris
     Cole Abrahams, and Burry Fredrik in association with S.
     Spencer Davids and Eddie Kulukundis.

LEADING ACTOR (PLAY)
Moses Gunn, *The Poison Tree*
George C. Scott, *Death of a Salesman*
Donald Sinden, *Habeas Corpus*
☆ John Wood, *Travesties*

LEADING ACTRESS (PLAY)
Tovah Feldshuh, *Yentl*
Rosemary Harris, *The Royal Family*
Lynn Redgrave, *Mrs. Warren's Profession*
☆ Irene Worth, *Sweet Bird of Youth*

FEATURED ACTOR (PLAY)
Barry Bostwick, *They Knew What They Wanted*
Gabriel Dell, *Lamppost Reunion*
☆ Edward Herrmann, *Mrs. Warren's Profession*
Daniel Seltzer, *Knock Knock*

FEATURED ACTRESS (PLAY)
Mary Beth Hurt, *Trelawny of the 'Wells'*
☆ Shirley Knight, *Kennedy's Children*
Lois Nettleton, *They Knew What They Wanted*
Meryl Streep, *27 Wagons Full of Cotton*

LEADING ACTOR (MUSICAL)
Mako, *Pacific Overtures*
Jerry Orbach, *Chicago*
Ian Richardson, *My Fair Lady*
☆ George Rose, *My Fair Lady*

LEADING ACTRESS (MUSICAL)
☆ Donna McKechnie, *A Chorus Line*
Vivian Reed, *Bubbling Brown Sugar*
Chita Rivera, *Chicago*
Gwen Verdon, *Chicago*

FEATURED ACTOR (MUSICAL)
Robert LuPone, *A Chorus Line*
Charles Repole, *Very Good Eddie*
Isao Sato, *Pacific Overtures*
☆ Sammy Williams, *A Chorus Line*

FEATURED ACTRESS (MUSICAL)
☆ Carole Bishop, *A Chorus Line*
Priscilla Lopez, *A Chorus Line*
Patti LuPone, *The Robber Bridegroom*

Virginia Seidel, *Very Good Eddie*

DIRECTOR (PLAY)

Arvin Brown, *Ah, Wilderness!*
Marshall W. Mason, *Knock Knock*
☆　Ellis Rabb, *The Royal Family*
Peter Wood, *Travesties*

DIRECTOR (MUSICAL)

☆　Michael Bennett, *A Chorus Line*
Bob Fosse, *Chicago*
Bill Gile, *Very Good Eddie*
Harold Prince, *Pacific Overtures*

BOOK (MUSICAL)

☆　*A Chorus Line* by James Kirkwood and Nicholas Dante
Chicago by Fred Ebb and Bob Fosse
Pacific Overtures by John Weidman
The Robber Bridegroom by Alfred Uhry

SCORE

☆　*A Chorus Line.* Music by Marvin Hamlisch, lyrics by Edward Kleban.
Chicago. Music by John Kander, lyrics by Fred Ebb.
Pacific Overtures. Music and lyrics by Stephen Sondheim.
Treemonisha. Music and lyrics by Scott Joplin.

SCENIC DESIGNER

☆　Boris Aronson, *Pacific Overtures*
Ben Edwards, *A Matter of Gravity*
David Mitchell, *Trelawny of the 'Wells'*
Tony Walton, *Chicago*

COSTUME DESIGNER

Theoni V. Aldredge, *A Chorus Line*
☆　Florence Klotz, *Pacific Overtures*
Ann Roth, *The Royal Family*
Patricia Zipprodt, *Chicago*

LIGHTING DESIGNER

Ian Calderon, *Trelawny of the 'Wells'*
Jules Fisher, *Chicago*
☆　Tharon Musser, *A Chorus Line*
Tharon Musser, *Pacific Overtures*

CHOREOGRAPHER

☆　Michael Bennett and Bob Avian, *A Chorus Line*

Patricia Birch, *Pacific Overtures*
Bob Fosse, *Chicago*
Billy Wilson, *Bubbling Brown Sugar*

REGIONAL THEATRE
☆ The Arena Stage, Washington, D.C. This award takes note of the company's balanced program of distinguished revivals and a broad spectrum of new works and American premieres of important foreign plays.

SPECIAL AWARDS
☆ Circle in the Square, for twenty-five continuous years of quality productions.
☆ Richard Burton, *Equus*
☆ Mathilde Pincus, for outstanding service to the Broadway musical theatre.
☆ Thomas H. Fitzgerald (posthumous), to the gifted lighting technician of countless Broadway shows and many Tony telecasts.

1977

MUSICAL
☆ *Annie.* Produced by Lewis Allen, Mike Nichols, Irwin Meyer and Stephen R. Friedman.
Happy End. Produced by Michael Harvey and The Chelsea Theater Center.
I Love My Wife. Produced by Terry Allen Kramer and Harry Rigby in association with Joseph Kipness.
Side By Side By Sondheim. Produced by Harold Prince in association with Ruth Mitchell.

PLAY
For Colored Girls Who Have Considered Suicide / When the Rainbow Is Enuf by Ntozake Shange. Produced by Joseph Papp.
☆ *The Shadow Box* by Michael Cristofer. Produced by Allan Francis, Ken Marsolais, Lester Osterman, and Leonard Soloway.
Otherwise Engaged by Simon Gray. Produced by Michael Codron, Frank Milton, and James M. Nederlander.
Streamers by David Rabe. Produced by Joseph Papp.

REVIVAL
Guys and Dolls. Produced by Moe Septee in association with Victor H. Potamkin, Carmen F. Zollo, and Ashton Springer.

☆ *Porgy and Bess.* Produced by Sherwin M. Goldman and Houston Grand Opera.
The Cherry Orchard. Produced by Joseph Papp.
Threepenny Opera. Produced by Joseph Papp.

LEADING ACTOR (PLAY)
Tom Courtenay, *Otherwise Engaged*
Ben Gazzara, *Who's Afraid of Virginia Woolf?*
☆ Al Pacino, *The Basic Training of Pavlo Hummel*
Ralph Richardson, *No Man's Land*

LEADING ACTRESS (PLAY)
Colleen Dewhurst, *Who's Afraid of Virginia Woolf?*
☆ Julie Harris, *The Belle of Amherst*
Liv Ullmann, *Anna Christie*
Irene Worth, *The Cherry Orchard*

FEATURED ACTOR (PLAY)
Bob Dishy, *Sly Fox*
Joe Fields, *The Basic Training of Pavlo Hummel*
Laurence Luckinbill, *The Shadow Box*
☆ Jonathan Pryce, *Comedians*

FEATURED ACTRESS (PLAY)
☆ Trazana Beverley, *For Colored Girls Who Have Considered Suicide / When the Rainbow Is Enuf*
Patricia Elliott, *The Shadow Box*
Rose Gregorio, *The Shadow Box*
Mary McCarty, *Anna Christie*

LEADING ACTOR (MUSICAL)
☆ Barry Bostwick, *The Robber Bridegroom*
Robert Guillaume, *Guys and Dolls*
Raul Julia, *Threepenny Opera*
Reid Shelton, *Annie*

LEADING ACTRESS (MUSICAL)
Clamma Dale, *Porgy and Bess*
Ernestine Jackson, *Guys and Dolls*
☆ Dorothy Loudon, *Annie*
Andrea McArdle, *Annie*

FEATURED ACTOR (MUSICAL)
☆ Lenny Baker, *I Love My Wife*
David Kernan, *Side By Side By Sondheim*
Larry Marshall, *Porgy and Bess*

Ned Sherrin, *Side By Side By Sondheim*

FEATURED ACTRESS (MUSICAL)
Ellen Green, *Threepenny Opera*
☆ Delores Hall, *Your Arm's Too Short to Box with God*
Millicent Martin, *Side By Side By Sondheim*
Julie N. McKenzie, *Side By Side By Sondheim*

DIRECTOR (PLAY)
☆ Gordon Davidson, *The Shadow Box*
Ulu Grosbard, *American Buffalo*
Mike Nichols, *Comedians*
Mike Nichols, *Streamers*

DIRECTOR (MUSICAL)
Vinnette Carroll, *Your Arm's Too Short to Box with God*
Martin Charnin, *Annie*
Jack O'Brien, *Porgy and Bess*
☆ Gene Saks, *I Love My Wife*

BOOK (MUSICAL)
☆ *Annie* by Thomas Meehan
Happy End by Elisabeth Hauptmann, adaptation by Michael
    Feingold
I Love My Wife by Michael Stewart
Your Arm's Too Short to Box with God by Vinnette Carroll

SCORE
☆ *Annie*. Music by Charles Strouse, lyrics by Martin Charnin.
Godspell. Music and lyrics by Stephen Schwartz.
I Love My Wife. Music by Cy Coleman, lyrics by Michael Stewart.
Happy End. Music by Kurt Weill, lyrics by Bertolt Brecht. Adapted
    by Michael Feingold.

SCENIC DESIGNER
Santo Loquasto, *American Buffalo*
Santo Loquasto, *The Cherry Orchard*
☆ David Mitchell, *Annie*
Robert Randolph, *Porgy and Bess*

COSTUME DESIGNER
☆ Theoni V. Aldredge, *Annie*
Theoni V. Aldredge, *Threepenny Opera*
☆ Santo Loquasto, *The Cherry Orchard*
Nancy Potts, *Porgy and Bess*

LIGHTING DESIGNER

John Bury, *No Man's Land*
Pat Collins, *Threepenny Opera*
Neil Peter Jampolis, *The Innocents*
☆ Jennifer Tipton, *The Cherry Orchard*

CHOREOGRAPHER
Talley Beatty, *Your Arm's Too Short to Box with God*
Patricia Birch, *Music Is*
☆ Peter Gennaro, *Annie*
Onna White, *I Love My Wife*

REGIONAL THEATRE
☆ Mark Taper Forum / Center Theatre Group

SPECIAL AWARDS
☆ Lily Tomlin
☆ Barry Manilow
☆ Diana Ross
☆ National Theatre of the Deaf
☆ Equity Library Theatre

1978

MUSICAL
☆ *Ain't Misbehavin'*. Produced by Emanuel Azenberg, Dasha Epstein, The Shubert Organization, Jane Gaynor, and Ron Dante.
Dancin'. Produced by Jules Fisher, The Shubert Organization, and Columbia Pictures.
On the Twentieth Century. Produced by The Producers Circle 2, Inc. (Robert Fryer, Mary Lea Johnson, James Cresson, and Martin Richards), Joseph Harris, and Ira Bernstein.
Runaways. Produced by Joseph Papp.

PLAY
Chapter Two by Neil Simon. Produced by Emanuel Azenberg.
☆ *Da* by Hugh Leonard. Produced by Lester Ostermann, Marilyn Strauss, and Marc Howard.
Deathtrap by Ira Levin. Produced by Alfred De Liagre, Jr. and Roger L. Stevens.
The Gin Game by D.L. Coburn. Produced by The Shubert Organization, Hume Cronyn, and Mike Nichols.

REVIVAL
☆ *Dracula*. Produced by Jujamcyn Theatre, Elizabeth I. McCann,

Photo: Anita and Steve Shevett

JESSICA TANDY AND HUME CRONYN

John Wulp, Victor Lurie, Nelle Nugent, and Max
    Weitzenhoffer.
Tartuffe. Produced by Circle in the Square.
Timbuktu! Produced by Luther Davis.
A *Touch of the Poet*. Produced by Elliot Martin.

LEADING ACTOR (PLAY)
Hume Cronyn, *The Gin Game*
☆   Barnard Hughes, *Da*
Frank Langella, *Dracula*

Jason Robards, A *Touch of the Poet*

LEADING ACTRESS (PLAY)

Anne Bancroft, *Golda*
Anita Gillette, *Chapter Two*
Estelle Parsons, *Miss Margarida's Way*
☆   Jessica Tandy, *The Gin Game*

FEATURED ACTOR (PLAY)

Morgan Freeman, *The Mighty Gents*
Victor Garber, *Deathtrap*
Cliff Gorman, *Chapter Two*
☆   Lester Rawlins, *Da*

FEATURED ACTRESS (PLAY)

Starletta DuPois, *The Mighty Gents*
Swoosie Kurtz, *Tartuffe*
Marian Seldes, *Deathtrap*
☆   Ann Wedgeworth, *Chapter Two*

LEADING ACTOR (MUSICAL)

Eddie Bracken, *Hello, Dolly!*
☆   John Cullum, *On the Twentieth Century*
Barry Nelson, *The Act*
Gilbert Price, *Timbuktu!*

LEADING ACTRESS (MUSICAL)

Madeline Kahn, *On the Twentieth Century*
Eartha Kitt, *Timbuktu!*
☆   Liza Minnelli, *The Act*
Frances Sternhagen, *Angel*

FEATURED ACTOR (MUSICAL)

Steven Boockvor, *Working*
Wayne Cilento, *Dancin'*
Rex Everhart, *Working*
☆   Kevin Kline, *On the Twentieth Century*

FEATURED ACTRESS (MUSICAL)

☆   Nell Carter, *Ain't Misbehavin'*
Imogene Coca, *On the Twentieth Century*
Ann Reinking, *Dancin'*
Charlaine Woodard, *Ain't Misbehavin'*

DIRECTOR (PLAY)

☆   Melvin Bernhardt, *Da*
Robert Moore, *Deathtrap*

Mike Nichols, The Gin Game
Dennis Rosa, Dracula

DIRECTOR (MUSICAL)

Bob Fosse, Dancin'
☆   Richard Maltby, Jr., Ain't Misbehavin'
Harold Prince, On the Twentieth Century
Elizabeth Swados, Runaways

BOOK (MUSICAL)

A History of the American Film by Christopher Durang
☆   On the Twentieth Century by Betty Comden, and Adolph Green
Runaways by Elizabeth Swados
Working by Stephen Schwartz

SCORE

The Act. Music by John Kander, lyrics by Fred Ebb.
☆   On the Twentieth Century. Music by Cy Coleman, lyrics by Betty
      Comden and Adolph Green.
Runaways. Music and lyrics by Elizabeth Swados.
Working. Music and Lyrics by Craig Carnelia, Micki Grant, Mary
      Rodgers / Susan Birkenhead, Stephen Schwartz, and James
      Taylor.

SCENIC DESIGNER

Zack Brown, The Importance of Being Earnest
Edward Gorey, Dracula
David Mitchell, Working
☆   Robin Wagner, On the Twentieth Century

COSTUME DESIGNER

☆   Edward Gorey, Dracula
Halston, The Act
Geoffrey Holder, Timbuktu!
Willa Kim, Dancin'

LIGHTING DESIGNER

Jules Fisher, Beatlemania
☆   Jules Fisher, Dancin'
Tharon Musser, The Act
Ken Billington, Working

CHOREOGRAPHER

Arthur Faria, Ain't Misbehavin'
☆   Bob Fosse, Dancin'
Ron Lewis, The Act
Elizabeth Swados, Runaways

REGIONAL THEATRE
☆ The Long Wharf Theatre, New Haven, Connecticut

1979

MUSICAL
Ballroom. Produced by Michael Bennett, Bob Avian, Bernard
Gersten, and Susan MacNair.
☆ *Sweeney Todd*. Produced by Richard Barr, Charles Woodward,
Robert Fryer, Mary Lea Johnson, and Martin Richards.
The Best Little Whorehouse in Texas. Produced by Universal Pictures.
They're Playing Our Song. Produced by Emanuel Azenberg.

PLAY
Bedroom Farce by Alan Ayckbourn. Produced by Robert Whitehead,
Roger L. Stevens, George W. George, and Frank Milton.
☆ *The Elephant Man* by Bernard Pomerance. Produced by
Richmond Crinkley, Elizabeth I. McCann, and Nelle Nugent.
Whose Life Is It Anyway? by Brian Clark. Produced by Emanuel
Azenberg, James Nederlander, and Ray Cooney.
Wings by Arthur Kopit. Produced by The Kennedy Center.

LEADING ACTOR (PLAY)
Philip Anglim, *The Elephant Man*
☆ Tom Conti, *Whose Life Is It Anyway?*
Jack Lemmon, *Tribute*
Alec McCowen, *St. Mark's Gospel*

LEADING ACTRESS (PLAY)
Jane Alexander, *First Monday in October*
☆ Constance Cummings, *Wings*
☆ Carole Shelley, *The Elephant Man*
Frances Sternhagen, *On Golden Pond*

FEATURED ACTOR (PLAY)
Bob Balaban, *The Inspector General*
☆ Michael Gough, *Bedroom Farce*
Joseph Maher, *Spokesong*
Edward James Olmos, *Zoot Suit*

FEATURED ACTRESS (PLAY)
☆ Joan Hickson, *Bedroom Farce*
Laurie Kennedy, *Man and Superman*
Susan Littler, *Bedroom Farce*

Photo: CBS Photography

ANGELA LANSBURY

Mary-Joan Negro, *Wings*

LEADING ACTOR (MUSICAL)
☆ Len Cariou, *Sweeney Todd*
Vincent Gardenia, *Ballroom*

Joel Grey, The Grand Tour
Robert Klein, They're Playing Our Song

LEADING ACTRESS (MUSICAL)
Tovah Feldshuh, Sarava
☆ Angela Lansbury, Sweeney Todd
Dorothy Loudon, Ballroom
Alexis Smith, Platinum

FEATURED ACTOR (MUSICAL)
Richard Cox, Platinum
☆ Henderson Forsythe, The Best Little Whorehouse in Texas
Gregory Hines, Eubie!
Ron Holgate, The Grand Tour

FEATURED ACTRESS (MUSICAL)
Joan Ellis, The Best Little Whorehouse in Texas
☆ Carlin Glynn, The Best Little Whorehouse in Texas
Millicent Martin, King of Hearts
Maxine Sullivan, My Old Friends

DIRECTOR (PLAY)
Alan Ayckbourn and Peter Hall, Bedroom Farce
Paul Giovanni, The Crucifier of Blood
☆ Jack Hofsiss, The Elephant Man
Michael Lindsay-Hogg, Whose Life Is It Anyway?

DIRECTOR (MUSICAL)
Michael Bennett, Ballroom
Peter Masterson and Tommy Tune, The Best Little Whorehouse in Texas
Robert Moore, They're Playing Our Song
☆ Harold Prince, Sweeney Todd

BOOK (MUSICAL)
Ballroom by Jerome Kass
☆ Sweeney Todd by Hugh Wheeler
The Best Little Whorehouse in Texas by Larry L. King and Peter
    Masterson
They're Playing Our Song by Neil Simon

SCORE
Carmelina. Music by Burton Lane, lyrics by Alan Jay Lerner.
Eubie! Music by Eubie Blake, lyrics by Noble Sissle, Andy Razaf,
    F. E. Miller, Johnny Brandon, and Jim Europe.
☆ Sweeney Todd. Music and lyrics by Stephen Sondheim.
The Grand Tour. Music and lyrics by Jerry Herman.

SCENIC DESIGNER
Karl Eigsti, *Knockout*
David Jenkins, *The Elephant Man*
☆   Eugene Lee, *Sweeney Todd*
John Wulp, *The Crucifier of Blood*

COSTUME DESIGNER
Theoni V. Aldredge, *Ballroom*
☆   Franne Lee, *Sweeney Todd*
Ann Roth, *The Crucifier of Blood*
Julie Weiss, *The Elephant Man*

LIGHTING DESIGNER
Ken Billington, *Sweeney Todd*
Beverly Emmons, *The Elephant Man*
☆   Roger Morgan, *The Crucifer of Blood*
Tharon Musser, *Ballroom*

CHOREOGRAPHER
☆   Michael Bennett and Bob Avian, *Ballroom*
Henry Le Tang and Billy Wilson, *Eubie!*
Dan Siretta, *Whoopee!*
Tommy Tune, *The Best Little Whorehouse in Texas*

REGIONAL THEATRE
☆   American Conservatory Theater, San Francisco, California

SPECIAL AWARDS
☆   Henry Fonda
☆   Walter F. Diehl, an active force in advancing the well-being of
     the Broadway theatre and of theatre nationally as
     International President of Theatre Stage Employees and
     Moving Pictures Operators.
☆   Eugene O'Neill Memorial Theatre Center, Waterford,
     Connecticut

The 1980s

"**I**t was Mother's Day in Paris. I was thinking,
'What shall I get her?' And, it came . . . the most wonderful present, 'My Tony Award.' It was, for her, the
proudest moment of her daughter's life, and for me,
the happiest. I shall never forget this memorable
moment, and I want to thank you for making it possible."

Liliane Montevecchi
Featured Actress (Musical), *Nine*

"It's tough to get out there eight times a week—with
any creative consistency. The nightly post-show post-
mortems you have with yourself can be hazardous to
your health. There are a few things, however, that help
make the angst worthwhile. One is the nights when it
actually is good and you know it. Two is the nights
when it actually is good and the audience knows it.
Three is the night you win a Tony for it.

Joan Allen
Actress (Play), *Burn This*

GLENN CLOSE

1980

MUSICAL

A *Day in Hollywood* / A *Night in the Ukraine*. Produced by Alexander H. Cohen and Hildy Parks.

Barnum. Produced by Cy Coleman and Judy Gordon, Maurice Rosenfield, and Lois Rosenfield.

☆ *Evita*. Produced by Robert Stigwood.

Sugar Babies. Produced by Terry Allen Kramer and Harry Rigby.

PLAY

Bent by Martin Sherman. Produced by Jack Schlissel and Steven Steinlauf.

☆ *Children of a Lesser God* by Mark Medoff. Produced by Emanual Azenberg, The Shubert Organization, Dasha Epstein, and Ron Dante.

Home by Samm-Art Williams. Produced by Elizabeth I. McCann, Nelle Nugent, Gerald S. Krone, and Ray Larsen.

Talley's Folly by Lanford Wilson. Produced by Nancy Cooperstein, Porter Van Zandt, and Marc Howard.

REVIVAL

Major Barbara. Produced by Circle in the Square.

☆ *Morning's at Seven*. Produced by Elizabeth I. McCann, Nelle Nugent, and Ray Larson.

Peter Pan. Produced by Zev Bufman.

West Side Story. Produced by Gladys Rackmil, The John F. Kennedy Center for the Performing Arts, James M. Nederlander, and Ruth Mitchell.

LEADING ACTOR (PLAY)

Charles Brown, *Home*

Gerald Hiken, *Strider*

Judd Hirsch, *Talley's Folly*

☆ John Rubenstein, *Children of a Lesser God*

LEADING ACTRESS (PLAY)

Blythe Danner, *Betrayal*

☆ Phyllis Frelich, *Children of a Lesser God*

Maggie Smith, *Night and Day*

Anne Twomey, *Nuts*

FEATURED ACTOR (PLAY)

David Dukes, *Bent*

George Hearn, *Watch on the Rhine*

Earle Hyman, *The Lady from Dubuque*

Joseph Maher, Night and Day
☆ David Rounds, Morning's at Seven

FEATURED ACTRESS (PLAY)
Maureen Anderman, The Lady from Dubuque
Pamela Burrell, Strider
Lois deBanzie, Morning's at Seven
☆ Dinah Manoff, I Ought to Be in Pictures

LEADING ACTOR (MUSICAL)
☆ Jim Dale, Barnum
Gregory Hines, Comin' Uptown
Mickey Rooney, Sugar Babies
Giorgio Tozzi, The Most Happy Fella

LEADING ACTRESS (MUSICAL)
Christine Andreas, Oklahoma!
Sandy Duncan, Peter Pan
☆ Patti LuPone, Evita
Ann Miller, Sugar Babies

FEATURED ACTOR (MUSICAL)
David Garrison, A Day in Hollywood / A Night in the Ukraine
Harry Groener, Oklahoma!
Bob Gunton, Evita
☆ Mandy Patinkin, Evita

FEATURED ACTRESS (MUSICAL)
Debbie Allen, West Side Story
Glenn Close, Barnum
Jossie DeGuzman, West Side Story
☆ Priscilla Lopez, A Day in Hollywood / A Night in the Ukraine

DIRECTOR (PLAY)
Gordon Davidson, Children of a Lesser God
Peter Hall, Betrayal
Marshall W. Mason, Talley's Folly
☆ Vivian Matalon, Morning's at Seven

DIRECTOR (MUSICAL)
Ernest Flatt and Rudy Tronto, Sugar Babies
Joe Layton, Barnum
☆ Harold Prince, Evita
Tommy Tune, A Day in Hollywood / A Night in the Ukraine

BOOK (MUSICAL)
A Day in Hollywood / A Night in the Ukraine by Dick Vosburgh

Barnum by Mark Bramble
☆   *Evita* by Tim Rice
Sugar Babies by Ralph G. Allen and Harry Rigby

SCORE

A Day in Hollywood / A Night in the Ukraine. Music by Frank Lazarus, lyrics by Dick Vosburgh.
Barnum. Music by Cy Coleman, lyrics by Michael Stewart.
☆   *Evita.* Music by Andrew Lloyd Webber, lyrics by Tim Rice.
Sugar Babies. Music and lyrics by Arthur Malvin.

SCENIC DESIGNER

☆   John Lee Beatty, *Talley's Folly*
☆   David Mitchell, *Barnum*
Timothy O'Brien and Tazeena Firth, *Evita*
Tony Walton, *A Day in Hollywood / A Night in the Ukraine*

COSTUME DESIGNER

☆   Theoni V. Aldredge, *Barnum*
Pierre Balmain, *Happy New Year*
Timothy O'Brien and Tazeena Firth, *Evita*
Raoul Péne du Bois, *Sugar Babies*

LIGHTING DESIGNER

Beverly Emmons, *A Day in Hollywood / A Night in the Ukraine*
☆   David Hersey, *Evita*
Craig Miller, *Barnum*
Dennis Parichy, *Talley's Folly*

CHOREOGRAPHER

Ernest Flatt, *Sugar Babies*
Larry Fuller, *Evita*
Joe Layton, *Barnum*
☆   Tommy Tune and Thommie Walsh, *A Day in Hollywood / A Night in the Ukraine*

REGIONAL THEATRE

☆   Actors Theatre of Louisville, Kentucky

SPECIAL AWARDS

☆   Mary Tyler Moore, *Whose Life Is It Anyway?*
☆   Goodspeed Opera House, East Haddam, Connecticut

1981

MUSICAL

☆ 42*nd* *Street*. Produced by David Merrick.

Sophisticated Ladies. Produced by Roger S. Berlind, Manheim Fox, Sondra Gilman, Burton L. Litwin, Louise Westergaard, Belwin Mills Publishing Corporation, and Norzar Productions, Inc.

Tintypes. Produced by Richmond Crinkley, Royal Pardon Productions, Ivan Bloch, Larry J. Silva, Eve Skina, and Joan F. Tobin.

Woman of the Year. Produced by Lawrence Kasha, David S. Landay, James M. Nederlander, Warner Theatre Productions, Claire Nichtern, Carole J. Shorenstein, and Stewart F. Lane.

PLAY

A *Lesson From Aloes* by Athol Fugard. Produced by Jay J. Cohen, Richard Press, Louis Bush Hager Associates in association with Yale Repertory Theatre, Lloyd Richards, Artistic Director.

A *Life* by Hugh Leonard. Produced by Lester Osterman, Richard Horner, Hinks Shimberg, and Freydberg-Cutler-Diamond Productions.

☆ *Amadeus* by Peter Shaffer. Produced by The Shubert Organization, Elizabeth I. McCann, Nelle Nugent, and Roger S. Berlind.

Fifth of July by Lanford Wilson. Produced by Jerry Arrow, Robert Lussier, and Warner Theatre Productions.

REVIVAL

Brigadoon. Produced by Zev Bufman and The Shubert Organization.

Camelot. Produced by Mike Merrick and Don Gregory.

The Little Foxes. Produced by Zev Bufman, Donald C. Carter, and Jon Cutler.

☆ *The Pirates of Penzance*. Produced by Joseph Papp and The New York Shakespeare Festival.

LEADING ACTOR (PLAY)

Tim Curry, *Amadeus*

Roy Dotrice, *A Life*

☆ Ian McKellen, *Amadeus*

Jack Weston, *The Floating Light Bulb*

LEADING ACTRESS (PLAY)

Glenda Jackson, *Rose*
☆ Jane Lapotaire, *Piaf*
Eva Le Gallienne, *To Grandmother's House We Go*
Elizabeth Taylor, *The Little Foxes*

FEATURED ACTOR (PLAY)

Tom Aldredge, *The Little Foxes*
☆ Brian Backer, *The Floating Light Bulb*
Adam Redfield, *A Life*
Shepperd Strudwick, *To Grandmother's House We Go*

FEATURED ACTRESS (PLAY)

☆ Swoosie Kurtz, *Fifth of July*
Maureen Stapleton, *The Little Foxes*
Jessica Tandy, *Rose*
Zoë Wanamaker, *Piaf*

LEADING ACTOR (MUSICAL)

Gregory Hines, *Sophisticated Ladies*
☆ Kevin Kline, *The Pirates of Penzance*
George Rose, *The Pirates of Penzance*
Martin Vidnovic, *Brigadoon*

LEADING ACTRESS (MUSICAL)

☆ Lauren Bacall, *Woman of the Year*
Meg Bussert, *Brigadoon*
Chita Rivera, *Bring Back Birdie*
Linda Ronstadt, *The Pirates of Penzance*

FEATURED ACTOR (MUSICAL)

Tony Azito, *The Pirates of Penzance*
☆ Hinton Battle, *Sophisticated Ladies*
Lee Roy Reams, *42nd Street*
Paxton Whitehead, *Camelot*

FEATURED ACTRESS (MUSICAL)

☆ Marilyn Cooper, *Woman of the Year*
Phyllis Hyman, *Sophisticated Ladies*
Wanda Richert, *42nd Street*
Lynne Thigpen, *Tintypes*

DIRECTOR (PLAY)

Peter Coe, *A Life*
☆ Peter Hall, *Amadeus*
Marshall W. Mason, *Fifth of July*
Austin Pendleton, *The Little Foxes*

DIRECTOR (MUSICAL)

Gower Champion, *42nd Street*
☆ Wilford Leach, T*he Pirates of Penzance*
Robert Moore, *Woman of the Year*
Michael Smuin, *Sophisticated Ladies*

BOOK (MUSICAL)

42nd Street by Michael Stewart and Mark Bramble
The Moony Shapiro Songbook by Monty Norman and Julian More
Tintypes by Mary Kyte
☆ *Woman of the Year* by Peter Stone

SCORE

Charlie and Algernon. Music by Charles Strouse, lyrics by David Rogers.
Copperfield. Music and lyrics by Al Kasha and Joel Hirschhorn.
Shakespeare's Cabaret. Music by Lance Mulcahy.
☆ *Woman of the Year.* Music by John Kander, lyrics by Fred Ebb.

SCENIC DESIGNER

John Lee Beatty, *Fifth of July*
☆ John Bury, *Amadeus*
Santo Loquasto, *The Suicide*
David Mitchell, *Can-Can*

COSTUME DESIGNER

Theoni V. Aldredge, *42nd Street*
John Bury, *Amadeus*
☆ Willa Kim, *Sophisticated Ladies*
Franca Squarciapino, *Can-Can*

LIGHTING DESIGNER

☆ John Bury, *Amadeus*
Tharon Musser, *42nd Street*
Dennis Parichy, *Fifth of July*
Jennifer Tipton, *Sophisticated Ladies*

CHOREOGRAPHER

☆ Gower Champion, *42nd Street*
Graciela Daniele, *The Pirates of Penzance*
Henry Le Tang, Donald McKayle, and Michael Smuin, *Sophisticated Ladies*
Roland Petit, *Can-Can*

REGIONAL THEATRE

☆ Trinity Square Repertory Company, Providence, Rhode Island

SPECIAL AWARD

☆ Lena Horne, for *Lena Horne: The Lady and Her Music*

1982

MUSICAL

Dreamgirls. Produced by Michael Bennett, Bob Avian, Geffen Records, and The Shubert Organization.

Joseph and the Amazing Technicolor Dreamcoat. Produced by Zev Bufman, Susan R. Rose, Melvin J. Estrin, Sidney Shlenker, and Gail Berman.

☆ *Nine*. Produced by Michel Stuart, Harvey J. Klaris, Roger S. Berlind, James M. Nederlander, Francine LeFrak, and Kenneth D. Greenblatt.

Pump Boys and Dinettes. Produced by Dodger Productions, Louis Busch Hager, Marilyn Strauss, Kate Studley, Warner Theater Productions Inc., and Max Weitzenhoffer.

PLAY

Crimes of the Heart by Beth Henley. Produced by Warner Theatre Productions Inc., Claire Nichtern, Mary Lea Johnson, Martin Richards, and Francine LeFrak.

The Dresser by Ronald Harwood. Produced by James M. Nederlander, Elizabeth I. McCann, Nelle Nugent, Warner Theater Productions, Inc., and Michael Codron.

'Master Harold'. . . and the Boys by Athol Fugard. Produced by The Shubert Organization, Freydberg/Bloch Productions, Dasha Epstein, Emanuel Azenberg, and David Geffen.

☆ *The Life and Adventures of Nicholas Nickleby* by David Edgar. Produced by James M. Nederlander, The Shubert Organization, Elizabeth I. McCann, and Nelle Nugent.

REVIVAL

A Taste of Honey. Produced by Roundabout Theatre Co., Gene Feist, and Michael Fried.

Medea. Produced by Barry and Fran Weissler, The Kennedy Center, and Bunny and Warren Austin.

My Fair Lady. Produced by Mike Merrick and Don Gregory.

☆ *Othello*. Produced by Barry and Fran Weissler and CBS Video Enterprises.

LEADING ACTOR (PLAY)

Tom Courtenay, *The Dresser*
Milo O'Shea, *Mass Appeal*

Christopher Plummer, *Othello*
☆ Roger Rees, *The Life and Adventures of Nicholas Nickleby*

LEADING ACTRESS (PLAY)
☆ Zoe Caldwell, *Medea*
Katharine Hepburn, *The West Side Waltz*
Geraldine Page, *Agnes of God*
Amanda Plummer, *A Taste of Honey*

FEATURED ACTOR (PLAY)
Richard Kavanaugh, *The Hothouse*
☆ Zakes Mokae, *'Master Harold'. . . and the Boys*
Edward Petherbridge, *The Life and Adventures of Nicholas Nickleby*
David Threlfall, *The Life and Adventures of Nicholas Nickleby*

FEATURED ACTRESS (PLAY)
Judith Anderson, *Medea*
Mia Dillon, *Crimes of the Heart*
Mary Beth Hurt, *Crimes of the Heart*
☆ Amanda Plummer, *Agnes of God*

LEADING ACTOR (MUSICAL)
Herschel Bernardi, *Fiddler on the Roof*
Victor Garber, *Little Me*
☆ Ben Harney, *Dreamgirls*
Raul Julia, *Nine*

LEADING ACTRESS (MUSICAL)
☆ Jennifer Holliday, *Dreamgirls*
Lisa Mordente, *Marlowe*
Mary Gordon Murray, *Little Me*
Sheryl Lee Ralph, *Dreamgirls*

FEATURED ACTOR (MUSICAL)
Obba Babatunde, *Dreamgirls*
☆ Cleavant Derricks, *Dreamgirls*
David Alan Grier, *The First*
Bill Hutton, *Joseph and the Amazing Technicolor Dreamcoat*

FEATURED ACTRESS (MUSICAL)
Karen Akers, *Nine*
Laurie Beechman, *Joseph and the Amazing Technicolor Dreamcoat*
☆ Liliane Montevecchi, *Nine*
Anita Morris, *Nine*

DIRECTOR (PLAY)
Melvin Bernhardt, *Crimes of the Heart*

Geraldine Fitzgerald, *Mass Appeal*
Athol Fugard, *'Master Harold'. . . and the Boys*
☆   Trevor Nunn / John Caird, *The Life and Adventures of Nicholas Nickleby*

DIRECTOR (MUSICAL)
Michael Bennett, *Dreamgirls*
Martin Charnin, *The First*
Tony Tanner, *Joseph and the Amazing Technicolor Dreamcoat*
☆   Tommy Tune, *Nine*

BOOK (MUSICAL)
☆   *Dreamgirls* by Tom Eyen
Joseph and the Amazing Technicolor Dreamcoat by Tim Rice
Nine by Arthur Kopit
The First by Joel Siegel and Martin Charnin

SCORE
Dreamgirls. Music by Henry Krieger, lyrics by Tom Eyen.
Joseph and the Amazing Technicolor Dreamcoat. Music by Andrew Lloyd
    Webber, lyrics by Tim Rice.
Merrily We Roll Along. Music and lyrics by Stephen Sondheim.
☆   *Nine.* Music and lyrics by Maury Yeston.

SCENIC DESIGNER
Ben Edwards, *Medea*
Lawrence Miller, *Nine*
☆   John Napier / Dermot Hayes, *The Life and Adventures of Nicholas Nickleby*
Robin Wagner, *Dreamgirls*

COSTUME DESIGNER
Theoni V. Aldredge, *Dreamgirls*
Jane Greenwood, *Medea*
☆   William Ivey Long, *Nine*
John Napier, *The Life and Adventures of Nicholas Nickleby*

LIGHTING DESIGNER
Martin Aronstein, *Medea*
David Hersey, *The Life and Adventures of Nicholas Nickleby*
Marcia Madeira, *Nine*
☆   Tharon Musser, *Dreamgirls*

CHOREOGRAPHER
☆   Michael Bennett / Michael Peters, *Dreamgirls*
Peter Gennaro, *Little Me*
Tony Tanner, *Joseph and the Amazing Technicolor Dreamcoat*

Tommy Tune, N*ine*
REGIONAL THEATRE
☆ The Guthrie Theatre, Minneapolis, Minnesota
SPECIAL AWARD
☆ The Actors' Fund of America

1983

MUSICAL
B*lues in the Night*. Produced by Mitchell Maxwell, Alan J. Schuster, Fred H. Krones, and M² Entertainment, Inc.
☆ *Cats*. Produced by Cameron Mackintosh, The Really Useful Company, Inc., David Geffen, and The Shubert Organization.
Merlin. Produced by Ivan Reitman, Columbia Pictures Stage Productions Inc., Marvin A. Krauss, and James M. Nederlander.
My One and Only. Produced by Paramount Theatre Productions, Francine LeFrak, and Kenneth- Mark Productions.

PLAY
A*ngels Fall* by Lanford Wilson. Produced by Elliot Martin, Circle Repertory Co., Lucille Lortel, The Shubert Organization, and The Kennedy Center.
'*Night, Mother* by Marsha Norman. Produced by Dann Byck, Wendell Cherry, The Shubert Organization, and Frederick M. Zollo.
Plenty by David Hare. Produced by Joseph Papp.
☆ *Torch Song Trilogy* by Harvey Fierstein. Produced by Kenneth Waissman, Martin Markinson, Lawrence Lane, John Glines, BetMar, and Donald Tick.

REVIVAL
All's Well That Ends Well. Produced by the Royal Shakespeare Company.
A View from the Bridge. Produced by Zev Bufman and Sidney Schlenker.
The Caine Mutiny Court-Martial. Produced by Circle in the Square Theatre and The Kennedy Center for the Performing Arts.
☆ *On Your Toes*. Produced by Alfred de Liagre, Jr., Roger L. Stevens, John Mauceri, Donald R. Seawell, and Andre Pastoria.

LEADING ACTOR (PLAY)
Jeffrey DeMunn, K2
☆ Harvey Fierstein, *Torch Song Trilogy*
Edward Herrmann, *Plenty*
Tony Lo Bianco, A *View from the Bridge*

LEADING ACTRESS (PLAY)
Kathy Bates, *'Night, Mother*
Kate Nelligan, *Plenty*
Anne Pitoniak, *'Night, Mother*
☆ Jessica Tandy, *Foxfire*

FEATURED ACTOR (PLAY)
☆ Matthew Broderick, *Brighton Beach Memoirs*
Zeljko Ivanek, *Brighton Beach Memoirs*
George N. Martin, *Plenty*
Stephen Moore, *All's Well That Ends Well*

FEATURED ACTRESS (PLAY)
Elizabeth Franz, *Brighton Beach Memoirs*
Roxanne Hart, *Passion*
☆ Judith Ivey, *Steaming*
Margaret Tyzack, *All's Well That Ends Well*

LEADING ACTOR (MUSICAL)
Al Green, *Your Arm's Too Short to Box with God*
George Hearn, A *Doll's Life*
Michael V. Smartt, *Porgy and Bess*
☆ Tommy Tune, *My One and Only*

LEADING ACTRESS (MUSICAL)
☆ Natalia Makarova, *On Your Toes*
Lonette McKee, *Show Boat*
Chita Rivera, *Merlin*
Twiggy, *My One and Only*

FEATURED ACTOR (MUSICAL)
☆ Charles "Honi" Coles, *My One and Only*
Harry Groener, *Cats*
Stephen Hanan, *Cats*
Lara Teeter, *On Your Toes*

FEATURED ACTRESS (MUSICAL)
Christine Andreas, *On Your Toes*
☆ Betty Buckley, *Cats*
Karla Burns, *Show Boat*
Denny Dillon, *My One and Only*

DIRECTOR (PLAY)
Marshall W. Mason, Angels Falls
Tom Moore, 'Night Mother
Trevor Nunn, All's Wells That Ends Well
☆ Gene Saks, Brighton Beach Memoirs

DIRECTOR (MUSICAL)
Michael Kahn, Show Boat
☆ Trevor Nunn, Cats
Ivan Reitman, Merlin
Tommy Tune, Thommie Walsh, My One and Only

BOOK (MUSICAL)
A Doll's Life by Betty Comden and Adolph Green
☆ Cats by T.S. Eliot
Merlin by Richard Levinson and William Link
My One and Only by Peter Stone and Timothy S. Mayer

SCORE
A Doll's Life. Music by Larry Grossman, lyrics by Betty Comden
    and Adolph Green.
☆ Cats. Music by Andrew Lloyd Webber, lyrics by T.S. Eliot.
Merlin. Music by Elmer Bernstein, lyrics by Don Black.
Seven Brides for Seven Brothers. Music by Gene de Paul, Al Kasha,
    and Joel Hirschhorn, lyrics by Johnny Mercer, Al Kasha,
    and Joel Hirschhorn.

SCENIC DESIGNER
John Gunter, All's Well That Ends Well
☆ Ming Cho Lee, K2
David Mitchell, Foxfire
John Napier, Cats

COSTUME DESIGNER
Lindy Hemming, All's Well That Ends Well
☆ John Napier, Cats
Rita Ryack, My One and Only
Patricia Zipprodt, Alice in Wonderland

LIGHTING DESIGNER
Ken Billington, Foxfire
Robert Bryan, All's Well That Ends Well
☆ David Hersey, Cats
Allen Lee Hughes, K2

CHOREOGRAPHER
George Faison, Porgy and Bess

Gillian Lynne, *Cats*
Donald Saddler, *On Your Toes*
☆ Tommy Tune, Thommie Walsh, *My One and Only*

REGIONAL THEATRE
☆ Oregon Shakespeare Festival Association, Ashland, Oregon

1984

MUSICAL
Baby. Produced by James B. Freydberg, Ivan Bloch, Kenneth-John Productions, Suzanne J. Schwartz, and Manuscript Productions.
☆ *La Cage aux Folles*. Produced by Allan Carr, Kenneth D. Greenblatt, Marvin A. Krauss, Steward F. Lane, James M. Nederlander, Martin Richards, Barry Brown, and Fritz Holt.
Sunday in the Park with George. Produced by The Shubert Organization and Emanuel Azenberg.
The Tap Dance Kid. Produced by Stanley White, Evelyn Barron, Harvey J. Klaris, and Michel Stuart.

PLAY
Glengarry Glen Ross by David Mamet. Produced by Elliot Martin, The Shubert Organization, Arnold Bernhard, and The Goodman Theatre.
Noises Off by Michael Frayn. Produced by James Nerderlander, Robert Fryer, Jerome Minskoff, The Kennedy Center, Michael Codron, Jonathan Farkas, and MTM Enterprises, Inc.
Play Memory by Joanna Glass. Produced by Alexander H. Cohen and Hildy Parks.
☆ *The Real Thing* by Tom Stoppard. Produced by Emanuel Azenburg, The Shubert Organization, Icarus Productions, Byron Goldman, Ivan Bloch, Roger Berlind, and Michael Codron.

REVIVAL
American Buffalo. Produced by Elliot Martin and Arnold Bernhard.
☆ *Death of a Salesman*. Produced by Robert Whitehead and Roger L. Stevens.
Heartbreak House. Produced by Circle in the Square.
A Moon for the Misbegotten. Produced by The Shubert Organization and Emanuel Azenberg.

ACTOR (PLAY)
☆ Jeremy Irons, *The Real Thing*
Calvin Levels, *Open Admissions*
Rex Harrison, *Heartbreak House*
Ian McKellen, *Ian McKellen Acting Shakespeare*

ACTRESS (PLAY)
☆ Glenn Close, *The Real Thing*
Rosemary Harris, *Heartbreak House*
Linda Hunt, *End of the World*
Kate Nelligan, *A Moon for the Misbegotten*

FEATURED ACTOR (PLAY)
Philip Bosco, *Heartbreak House*
☆ Joe Mantegna, *Glengarry Glen Ross*
Robert Prosky, *Glengarry Glen Ross*
Douglas Seale, *Noises Off*

FEATURED ACTRESS (PLAY)
☆ Christine Baraski, *The Real Thing*
Jo Henderson, *Play Memory*
Dana Ivey, *Heartbreak House*
Deborah Rush, *Noises Off*

ACTOR (MUSICAL)
Gene Barry, *La Cage aux Folles*
☆ George Hearn, *La Cage aux Folles*
Ron Moody, *Oliver!*
Mandy Patinkin, *Sunday in the Park with George*

ACTRESS (MUSICAL)
Rhetta Hughes, *Amen Corner*
Liza Minnelli, *The Rink*
Bernadette Peters, *Sunday in the Park with George*
☆ Chita Rivera, *The Rink*

FEATURED ACTOR (MUSICAL)
☆ Hinton Battle, *The Tap Dance Kid*
Stephen Geoffreys, *The Human Comedy*
Todd Graff, *Baby*
Samuel E. Wright, *The Tap Dance Kid*

FEATURED ACTRESS (MUSICAL)
Martine Allard, *The Tap Dance Kid*
Liz Callaway, *Baby*
Dana Ivey, *Sunday in the Park with George*

☆ Lila Kedrova, *Zorba*

DIRECTOR (PLAY)

Michael Blakemore, *Noises Off*
David Leveaux, *A Moon for the Misbegotten*
Gregory Mosher, *Glengarry Glen Ross*
☆ Mike Nichols, *The Real Thing*

DIRECTOR (MUSICAL)

James Lapine, *Sunday in the Park with George*
☆ Arthur Laurents, *La Cage aux Folles*
Richard Maltby Jr., *Baby*
Vivian Matalon, *The Tap Dance Kid*

BOOK (MUSICAL)

Baby by Sybille Pearson
☆ *La Cage aux Folles* by Harvey Fierstein
Sunday in the Park with George by James Lapine
The Tap Dance Kid by Charles Blackwell

SCORE

Baby. Music by David Shire, lyrics by Richard Maltby, Jr.
☆ *La Cage aux Folles.* Music and lyrics by Jerry Herman.
The Rink. Music by John Kander, lyrics by Fred Ebb.
Sunday in the Park with George. Music and lyrics by Stephen
    Sondheim.

SCENIC DESIGNER

Clarke Dunham, *End of the World*
Peter Larkin, *The Rink*
☆ Tony Straiges, *Sunday in the Park with George*
Tony Walton, *The Real Thing*

COSTUME DESIGNER

☆ Theoni V. Aldredge, *La Cage aux Folles*
Jane Greenwood, *Heartbreak House*
Anthea Sylbert, *The Real Thing*
Patricia Zipprodt and Ann Hould-Ward, *Sunday in the Park with
    George*

LIGHTING DESIGNER

Ken Billington, *End of the World*
Jules Fisher, *La Cage aux Folles*
☆ Richard Nelson, *Sunday in the Park with George*
Marc B. Weiss, *A Moon for the Misbegotten*

CHOREOGRAPHER
Wayne Cilento, *Baby*
Graciela Daniele, *The Rink*
☆ Danny Daniels, *The Tap Dance Kid*
Scott Salmon, *La Cage aux Folles*

REGIONAL THEATRE
☆ Old Globe Theatre, San Diego, California

SPECIAL AWARDS
☆ *La Tragedie de Carmen* for outstanding achievement in musical theatre.
☆ Peter Feller, for devoting forty years to theatre stagecraft and magic.
☆ A *Chorus Line* for becoming Broadway's longest running musical (Gold Tony).

1985

MUSICAL
☆ *Big River.* Produced by Rocco Landesman, Heidi Landesman, Rick Steiner, M. Anthony Fisher, and Dodger Productions.
Grind. Produced by Kenneth D. Greenblatt, John J. Pomerantz, Mary Lea Johnson, Martin Richards, James M. Nederlander, Harold Prince, Michael Frazier, Susan Madden Samson, and Jonathan Farkas.
Leader of the Pack. Produced by Elizabeth I. McCann, Nelle Nugent, Francine LeFrak, Clive Davis, John Hart Associates, Inc., Rodger Hess, and Richard Kagan.
Quilters. Produced by The Denver Center for the Performing Arts, The John F. Kennedy Center for the Performing Arts, The American National Theatre and Academy, and Brockman Seawell.

PLAY
As Is by William M. Hoffman. Produced by John Glines / Lawrence Lane, Lucille Lortel, and The Shubert Organization.
☆ *Biloxi Blues* by Neil Simon. Produced by Emanuel Azenberg and the Center Theater Group / Ahmanson Theatre, Los Angeles.
Hurlyburly by David Rabe. Produced by Icarus Productions, Frederick M. Zollo, Ivan Bloch, and ERB Productions.
Ma Rainey's Black Bottom by August Wilson. Produced by Ivan Bloch, Robert Cole, and Frederick M. Zollo.

REVIVAL

Cyrano de Bergerac. Produced by James M. Nederlander, Elizabeth I. McCann, Nelle Nugent, Cynthia Wood, Dale Duffy, and Allan Carr.

☆ *Joe Egg.* Produced by The Shubert Organization, Emanuel Azenberg, Roger Berlind, Ivan Bloch, and MTM Enterprises, Inc.

Much Ado About Nothing. Produced by James M. Nederlander, Elizabeth I. McCann, Nelle Nugent, Cynthia Wood, Dale Duffy, and Allan Carr.

Strange Interlude. Produced by Robert Michael Geisler, John Roberdeau, Douglas Urbanski, James M. Nederlander, Duncan C. Weldon, Paul Gregg, Lionel Becker, and Jerome Minskoff.

ACTOR (PLAY)

Jim Dale, *Joe Egg*

Jonathan Hogan, *As Is*

☆ Derek Jacobi, *Much Ado About Nothing*

John Lithgow, *Requiem for a Heavyweight*

ACTRESS (PLAY)

☆ Stockard Channing, *Joe Egg*

Sinead Cusack, *Much Ado About Nothing*

Rosemary Harris, *Pack of Lies*

Glenda Jackson, *Strange Interlude*

FEATURED ACTOR (PLAY)

Charles S. Dutton, *Ma Rainey's Black Bottom*

William Hurt, *Hurlyburly*

☆ Barry Miller, *Biloxi Blues*

Edward Petherbridge, *Strange Interlude*

FEATURED ACTRESS (PLAY)

Joanna Gleason, *Joe Egg*

☆ Judith Ivey, *Hurlyburly*

Theresa Merritt, *Ma Rainey's Black Bottom*

Sigourney Weaver, *Hurlyburly*

ACTOR (MUSICAL)

Category eliminated

ACTRESS (MUSICAL)

Category eliminated

FEATURED ACTOR (MUSICAL)

René Auberjonois, *Big River*

Daniel H. Jenkins, B*ig River*
Kurt Knudson, T*ake Me Along*
☆ Ron Richardson, B*ig River*

FEATURED ACTRESS (MUSICAL)
Evalyn Baron, *Quilters*
☆ Leilani Jones, *Grind*
Mary Beth Peil, T*he King and* I
Lenka Peterson, *Quilters*

DIRECTOR (PLAY)
Keith Hack, S*trange Interlude*
Terry Hands, *Much Ado About Nothing*
Marshall W. Mason, A*s Is*
☆ Gene Saks, B*iloxi Blues*

DIRECTOR (MUSICAL)
Barbara Damashek, *Quilters*
Mitch Leigh, T*he King and* I
☆ Des McAnuff, B*ig River*
Harold Prince, *Grind*

BOOK (MUSICAL)
☆ B*ig River* by William Hauptman
Grind by Fay Kanin
Harrigan 'n Hart by Michael Stewart
Quilters by Molly Newman and Barbara Damashek

SCORE
☆ B*ig River.* Music and lyrics by Roger Miller.
Grind. Music by Larry Grossman and lyrics by Ellen Fitzhugh.
Quilters. Music and lyrics by Barbara Damashek.

SCENIC DESIGNER
Clarke Dunham, *Grind*
Ralph Koltai, M*uch Ado About Nothing*
☆ Heidi Landesman, B*ig River*
Voytek and Michael Levine, S*trange Interlude*

COSTUME DESIGNER
☆ Florence Klotz, *Grind*
Patricia McGourty, B*ig River*
Alexander Reid, C*yrano de Bergerac*
Alexander Reid, M*uch Ado About Nothing*

LIGHTING DESIGNER
Terry Hands, C*yrano de Bergerac*

Terry Hands, Much Ado About Nothing
Allen Lee Hughes, Strange Interlude
☆ Richard Riddell, Big River

CHOREOGRAPHER
Category eliminated

REGIONAL THEATRE
☆ Steppenwolf Theatre Company, Chicago, Illinois

SPECIAL AWARDS
☆ Yul Brynner, honoring his 4,525 performances in The King and I
☆ New York State Council on the Arts

1986

MUSICAL
Big Deal. Produced by The Shubert Organization, Roger Berlind,
    Jerome Minskoff, and Jonathan Farkas.
☆ The Mystery of Edwin Drood. Produced by Joseph Papp.
Song & Dance. Produced by Cameron Mackintosh, Inc., The
    Shubert Organization, F.W.M. Producing Group, and The
    Really Useful Company, Inc.
Tango Argentino. Produced by Mel Howard and Donald K. Donald.

PLAY
Benefactors by Michael Frayn. Produced by James M. Nederlander,
    Robert Fryer, Douglas Urbanski, Michael Codron, MTM
    Enterprises, Inc., and CBS Productions.
Blood Knot by Athol Fugard. Produced by James B. Freydberg,
    Max Weitzenhoffer, Lucille Lortel, Estrin Rose Berman
    Productions, and F.W.M. Producing Group.
The House of Blue Leaves by John Guare. Produced by Lincoln
    Center Theater, Gregory Mosher, and Bernard Gersten.
☆ I'm Not Rappaport by Herb Gardner. Produced by James
    Walsh, Lewis Allen, and Martin Heinfling.

REVIVAL
Hay Fever. Produced by Roger Peters and MBS Co.
The Iceman Cometh. Produced by Lewis Allen, James M.
    Nederlander, Stephen Graham, and Ben Edwards.
Loot. Produced by The David Merrick Arts Foundation, Charles P.
    Kopelman, and Mark Simon.
☆ Sweet Charity. Produced by Jerome Minskoff, James M.
    Nederlander, Arthur Rubin, and Joseph Harris.

ACTOR (PLAY)

Hume Cronyn, The Petition
Ed Harris, Precious Sons
☆ Judd Hirsch, I'm Not Rappaport
Jack Lemmon, Long Day's Journey Into Night

ACTRESS (PLAY)

Rosemary Harris, Hay Fever
Mary Beth Hurt, Benefactors
Jessica Tandy, The Petition
☆ Lily Tomlin, The Search for Signs of Intelligent Life in the Universe

FEATURED ACTOR (PLAY)

Peter Gallagher, Long Day's Journey Into Night
Charles Keating, Loot
Joseph Maher, Loot
☆ John Mahoney, The House of Blue Leaves

FEATURED ACTRESS (PLAY)

Stockard Channing, The House of Blue Leaves
☆ Swoosie Kurtz, The House of Blue Leaves
Bethel Leslie, Long Day's Journey Into Night
Zoë Wanamaker, Loot

ACTOR (MUSICAL)

Don Correia, Singin' in the Rain
Cleavant Derricks, Big Deal
Maurice Hines, Uptown . . . It's Hot!
☆ George Rose, The Mystery of Edwin Drood

ACTRESS (MUSICAL)

Debbie Allen, Sweet Charity
Cleo Laine, The Mystery of Edwin Drood
☆ Bernadette Peters, Song & Dance
Chita Rivera, Jerry's Girls

FEATURED ACTOR (MUSICAL)

Christopher d'Ambroise, Song & Dance
John Herrera, The Mystery of Edwin Drood
Howard McGillin, The Mystery of Edwin Drood
☆ Michael Rupert, Sweet Charity

FEATURED ACTRESS (MUSICAL)

Patti Cohenour, The Mystery of Edwin Drood
☆ Bebe Neuwirth, Sweet Charity
Jana Schneider, The Mystery of Edwin Drood
Elisabeth Welch, Jerome Kern Goes to Hollywood

Photo: Anita and Steve Shevett

SARAH JESSICA PARKER, BERNADETTE PETERS,
AND MATTHEW BRODERICK

DIRECTOR (PLAY)
Jonathan Miller, *Long Day's Journey Into Night*
José Quintero, *The Iceman Cometh*
John Tillinger, *Loot*
☆ Jerry Zaks, *The House of Blue Leaves*

DIRECTOR (MUSICAL)
Bob Fosse, *Big Deal*
☆ Wilford Leach, *The Mystery of Edwin Drood*
Richard Maltby Jr., *Song & Dance*
Claudio Segovia and Hector Orezzoli, *Tango Argentino*

BOOK (MUSICAL)
Big Deal by Bob Fosse
☆ *The Mystery of Edwin Drood* by Rupert Holmes
Singin' in the Rain by Betty Comden and Adolph Green
Wind in the Willows by Jane Iredale

SCORE
☆ The Mystery of Edwin Drood, Rupert Holmes
The News, Paul Schierhorn
Song & Dance, Andrew Lloyd Webber, Don Black, and Richard Maltby, Jr.
Wind in the Willows, William Perry and Roger McGough

SCENIC DESIGNER
Ben Edwards, The Iceman Cometh
David Mitchell, The Boys in Winter
Beni Montresor, The Marriage of Figaro
☆ Tony Walton, The House of Blue Leaves

COSTUME DESIGNER
Willa Kim, Song & Dance
Beni Montresor, The Marriage of Figaro
Ann Roth, The House of Blue Leaves
☆ Patricia Zipprodt, Sweet Charity

LIGHTING DESIGNER
☆ Pat Collins, I'm Not Rappaport
Jules Fisher, Song & Dance
Paul Gallo, The House of Blue Leaves
Thomas R. Skelton, The Iceman Cometh

CHOREOGRAPHER
Graciela Daniele, The Mystery of Edwin Drood
☆ Bob Fosse, Big Deal
Peter Martins, Song & Dance
Tango Argentino Dancers, Tango Argentino

REGIONAL THEATRE
☆ American Repertory Theatre, Cambridge, Massachusetts.

1987

MUSICAL
☆ Les Misérables. Produced by Cameron Mackintosh.
Me and My Girl. Produced by Richard Armitage, Terry Allen Kramer, James M. Nederlander, and Stage Promotions Limited & Co.
Rags. Produced by Lee Guber, Martin Heinfling, and Marvin A. Krauss.
Starlight Express. Produced by Martin Starger and Lord Grade.

PLAY

Broadway Bound by Neil Simon. Produced by Emanuel Azenburg.
Coastal Disturbances by Tina Howe. Produced by Circle in the
Square, Theodore Mann, and Paul Libin.
☆ *Fences* by August Wilson. Produced by Carole Shorenstein
Hays and The Yale Repertory Theatre.
Les Liaisons Dangereuses by Christopher Hampton. Produced by
James M. Nederlander, The Shubert Organization, Inc.,
Jerome Minskoff, Elizabeth I. McCann, Stephen Graham,
and Jonathon Farkas.

REVIVAL

☆ *All My Sons*. Produced by Jay H. Fuchs, Steven Warnick, and
Charles Patsos.
The Front Page. Produced by Lincoln Center Theater, Gregory
Mosher, and Bernard Gersten.
The Life and Adventures of Nicholas Nickleby. Produced by The
Shubert Organization, Three Knights, Ltd., and Robert
Fox, Ltd.
Pygmalion. Produced by The Shubert Organization, Jerome
Minskoff, and Duncan C. Weldon.

ACTOR (PLAY)

Philip Bosco, *You Never Can Tell*
☆ James Earl Jones, *Fences*
Richard Kiley, *All My Sons*
Alan Rickman, *Les Liaisons Dangereuses*

ACTRESS (PLAY)

Lindsay Duncan, *Les Liaisons Dangereuses*
☆ Linda Lavin, *Broadway Bound*
Geraldine Page, *Blithe Spirit*
Amanda Plummer, *Pygmalion*

FEATURED ACTOR (PLAY)

Frankie R. Faison, *Fences*
☆ John Randolph, *Broadway Bound*
Jamey Sheridan, *All My Sons*
Courtney B. Vance, *Fences*

FEATURED ACTRESS (PLAY)

☆ Mary Alice, *Fences*
Annette Bening, *Coastal Disturbances*
Phyllis Newman, *Broadway Bound*
Carole Shelley, *Stepping Out*

ACTOR (MUSICAL)
Roderick Cook, Oh *Coward!*
☆ Robert Lindsay, Me *and My Girl*
Terrence Mann, Les *Misérables*
Colm Wilkinson, Les *Misérables*

ACTRESS (MUSICAL)
Catherine Cox, Oh *Coward!*
☆ Maryann Plunkett, Me *and My Girl*
Teresa Stratas, Rags

FEATURED ACTOR (MUSICAL)
George S. Irving, Me *and My Girl*
Timothy Jerome, Me *and My Girl*
☆ Michael Maguire, Les *Misérables*
Robert Torti, Starlight *Express*

FEATURED ACTRESS (MUSICAL)
Jane Connell, Me *and My Girl*
Judy Kuhn, Les *Misérables*
☆ Frances Ruffelle, Les *Misérables*
Jane Summerhays, Me *and My Girl*

DIRECTOR (PLAY)
Howard Davies, Les *Liaisons Dangereuses*
Mbongeni Ngema, Asinamali!
☆ Lloyd Richards, Fences
Carole Rothman, Coastal *Disturbances*

DIRECTOR (MUSICAL)
Brian MacDonald, The *Mikado*
☆ Trevor Nunn and John Caird, Les *Misérables*
Trevor Nunn, Starlight *Express*
Mike Ockrent, Me *and My Girl*

BOOK (MUSICAL)
☆ Les *Misérables* by Alain Boubil and Claude-Michel Schönberg
Me *and My Girl* by L. Arthur Rose, Douglas Furber, Stephen Fry,
and Mike Ockrent
Rags by Joseph Stein
Smile by Howard Ashman

SCORE
☆ Les *Misérables*. Music by Claude-Michel Schönberg, lyrics by
Herbert Kretzmer and Alain Boublil.
Me *and My Girl*. Music by Noel Gay, lyrics by L. Arthur Rose and
Douglas Furber.

Rags. Music by Charles Strouse, lyrics by Stephen Schwartz.
Starlight Express. Music by Andrew Lloyd Webber, lyrics by
Richard Stilgoe.

SCENIC DESIGNER
Bob Crowley, *Les Liaisons Dangereuses*
Martin Johns, *Me and My Girl*
☆ John Napier, *Les Misérables*
Tony Walton, *The Front Page*

COSTUME DESIGNER
Bob Crowley, *Les Liaisons Dangereuses*
Ann Curtis, *Me and My Girl*
☆ John Napier, *Starlight Express*
Andreane Neofitou, *Les Misérables*

LIGHTING DESIGNER
Martin Aronstein, *Wild Honey*
☆ David Hersey, *Les Misérables*
David Hersey, *Starlight Express*
Beverly Emmons and Chris Parry, *Les Liaisons Dangereuses*

CHOREOGRAPHER
Ron Field, *Rags*
☆ Gillian Gregory, *Me and My Girl*
Brian Macdonald, *The Mikado*
Arlene Phillips, *Starlight Express*

REGIONAL THEATRE
☆ San Francisco Mime Troupe, San Francisco, California

SPECIAL AWARDS
☆ George Abbott, on the occasion of his 100th birthday.
☆ Jackie Mason, for *The World According to Me.*

1988

MUSICAL
Into the Woods. Produced by Heidi Landesman, Rocco Landesman,
Rick Steiner, M. Anthony Fisher, Frederic H. Mayerson,
and Jujamcyn Theatres.
☆ *The Phantom of the Opera.* Produced by Cameron Mackintosh
and The Really Useful Theatre Company, Inc.
Romance / Romance. Produced by Dasha Epstein, Harve Brosten,
and Jay S. Bulmash.

Sarafina! Produced by Lincoln Center Theater, Gregory Mosher, Bernard Gersten, Lucille Lortel, and The Shubert Organization.

PLAY

A *Walk in the Woods* by Lee Blessing. Produced by Lucille Lortel, American Playhouse Theatre Productions, and Yale Repertory Theatre.

Joe Turner's Come and Gone by August Wilson. Produced by Elliot Martin, Vy Higginsen, Ken Wydro, and Yale Repertory Theatre.

☆   *M. Butterfly* by David Henry Hwang. Produced by Stuart Ostrow and David Geffen.

Speed-the-Plow by David Mamet. Produced by Lincoln Center Theater, Gregory Mosher, and Bernard Gersten.

REVIVAL

☆   *Anything Goes.* Produced by Lincoln Center Theater, Gregory Mosher, and Bernard Gersten.

A *Streetcar Named Desire.* Produced by Circle in the Square, Theodore Mann, and Paul Libin.

Cabaret, Produced by Barry Weissler and Fran Weissler.

Dreamgirls. Produced by Marvin A. Krauss and Irving Siders.

ACTOR (PLAY)

Derek Jacobi, *Breaking the Code*
John Lithgow, *M. Butterfly*
Robert Prosky, A *Walk in the Woods*
☆   Ron Silver, *Speed-the-Plow*

ACTRESS (PLAY)

☆   Joan Allen, *Burn This*
Blythe Danner, A *Streetcar Named Desire*
Glenda Jackson, *Macbeth*
Frances McDormand, A *Streetcar Named Desire*

FEATURED ACTOR (PLAY)

Michael Gough, *Breaking the Code*
Lou Liberatore, *Burn This*
Delroy Lindo, *Joe Turner's Come and Gone*
☆   B.D. Wong, *M. Butterfly*

FEATURED ACTRESS (PLAY)

Kimberleigh Aarn, *Joe Turner's Come and Gone*
☆   L. Scott Caldwell, *Joe Turner's Come and Gone*
Kate Nelligan, *Serious Money*

Kimberly Scott, *Joe Turner's Come and Gone*

ACTOR (MUSICAL)
Scott Bakula, *Romance / Romance*
David Carroll, *Chess*
☆   Michael Crawford, *The Phantom of the Opera*
Howard McGlllin, *Anything Goes*

ACTRESS (MUSICAL)
Alison Fraser, *Romance / Romance*
☆   Joanna Gleason, *Into the Woods*
Judy Kuhn, *Chess*
Patti LuPone, *Anything Goes*

FEATURED ACTOR (MUSICAL)
Anthony Heald, *Anything Goes*
Werner Klemperer, *Cabaret*
☆   Bill McCutcheon, *Anything Goes*
Robert Westenberg, *Into the Woods*

FEATURED ACTRESS (MUSICAL)
☆   Judy Kaye, *The Phantom of the Opera*
Leleti Khumalo, *Sarafina!*
Alyson Reed, *Cabaret*
Regina Resnik, *Cabaret*

DIRECTOR (PLAY)
☆   John Dexter, *M. Butterfly*
Gregory Mosher, *Speed-the-Plow*
Lloyd Richards, *Joe Turner's Come and Gone*
Clifford Williams, *Breaking the Code*

DIRECTOR (MUSICAL)
James Lapine, *Into the Woods*
Mbongeni Ngema, *Sarafina!*
☆   Harold Prince, *The Phantom of the Opera*
Jerry Zaks, *Anything Goes*

BOOK (MUSICAL)
The Gospel at Colonus by Lee Breuer
☆   *Into the Woods* by James Lapine
The Phantom of the Opera by Richard Stilgoe and Andrew Lloyd
     Webber
Romance / Romance by Barry Harman

SCORE
☆   *Into the Woods*. Music and lyrics by Stephen Sondheim.

The *Phantom of the Opera*. Music by Andrew Lloyd Webber, lyrics
by Charles Hart and Richard Stilgoe.
Romance / Romance. Music by Keith Herrmann, lyrics by Barry
Harman.
Sarafina! Music and lyrics by Mbongeni Ngema and Hugh
Masakela.

SCENIC DESIGNER
☆ Maria Björnson, *The Phantom of the Opera*
Eiko Ishioka, M. *Butterfly*
Tony Straiges, *Into the Woods*
Tony Walton, *Anything Goes*

COSTUME DESIGNER
☆ Maria Björnson, *The Phantom of the Opera*
Ann Hould-Ward, *Into the Woods*
Eiko Ishioka, M. *Butterfly*
Tony Walton, *Anything Goes*

LIGHTING DESIGNER
☆ Andrew Bridge, *The Phantom of the Opera*
Paul Gallo, *Anything Goes*
Richard Nelson, *Into the Woods*
Andy Phillips, M. *Butterfly*

CHOREOGRAPHER
Lar Lubovitch, *Into the Woods*
Gillian Lynne, *The Phantom of the Opera*
Ndaba Mhlongo and Mbongeni Ngema, *Sarafina!*
☆ Michael Smuin, *Anything Goes*

REGIONAL THEATRE
☆ South Coast Repertory of Costa Mesa, California

SPECIAL AWARDS
☆ Brooklyn Academy of Music

1989

MUSICAL
Black and Blue. Produced by Mel Howard and Donald K. Donald.
☆ *Jerome Robbins' Broadway*. Produced by The Shubert
Organization, Roger Berlind, Suntory Intertaional Corp.,
Byron Goldman, and Emanuel Azenberg.
Starmites. Produced by Hinks Shimberg, Mary Keil, and Steven
Warnick.

PLAY

Largely New York by Bill Irwin. Produced by James B. Freydberg, Kenneth Feld, Jerry L. Cohen, Max Weitzenhoffer, The John F. Kennedy Center for the Performing Arts, and The Walt Disney Studios.

Lend Me a Tenor by Ken Ludwig. Produced by Martin Starger and The Really Useful Theatre Company, Inc.

Shirley Valentine by Willy Russell. Produced by The Really Useful Theatre Company, Inc. and Bob Swash.

☆ *The Heidi Chronicles* by Wendy Wasserstein. Produced by The Shubert Organization, Suntory International Corp., James Walsh, and Playwrights Horizons.

REVIVAL

Ah, Wilderness! Produced by Ken Marsolais, Alexander H. Cohen, The Kennedy Center for the Performing Arts, Yale Repertory Theatre, Richard Norton, Irma Oestreicher, and Elizabeth D. White.

Ain't Misbehavin'. Produced by The Shubert Organization, Emanuel Azenberg, Dasha Epstein, and Roger Berlind.

Café Crown. Produced by LeFrak Entertainment, James M. Nederlander, Francine LeFrak, James L. Nederlander, and Arthur Rubin.

☆ *Our Town.* Produced by Lincoln Center Theater, Gregory Mosher, and Bernard Gersten.

ACTOR (PLAY)

Mikhail Baryshnikov, *Metamorphosis*
☆ Philip Bosco, *Lend Me a Tenor*
Victor Garber, *Lend Me a Tenor*
Bill Irwin, *Largely New York*

ACTRESS (PLAY)

Joan Allen, *The Heidi Chronicles*
☆ Pauline Collins, *Shirley Valentine*
Madeline Kahn, *Born Yesterday*
Kate Nelligan, *Spoils of War*

FEATURED ACTOR (PLAY)

Peter Frechette, *Eastern Standard*
☆ Boyd Gaines, *The Heidi Chronicles*
Eric Stoltz, *Our Town*
Gordon Joseph Weiss, *Ghetto*

FEATURED ACTRESS (PLAY)
☆ Christine Baranski, *Rumors*
Joanne Camp, *The Heidi Chronicles*
Tovah Feldshuh, *Lend Me a Tenor*
Penelope Ann Miller, *Our Town*

ACTOR (MUSICAL)
☆ Jason Alexander, *Jerome Robbins' Broadway*
Gabriel Barre, *Starmites*
Brian Lane Green, *Starmites*
Robert La Fosse, *Jerome Robbins' Broadway*

ACTRESS (MUSICAL)
☆ Ruth Brown, *Black and Blue*
Charlotte d'Amboise, *Jerome Robbins' Broadway*
Linda Hopkins, *Black and Blue*
Sharon McNight, *Starmites*

FEATURED ACTOR (MUSICAL)
Bunny Briggs, *Black and Blue*
Savion Glover, *Black and Blue*
Scott Wentworth, *Welcome to the Club*
☆ Scott Wise, *Jerome Robbins' Broadway*

FEATURED ACTRESS (MUSICAL)
Jane Lanier, *Jerome Robbins' Broadway*
Faith Prince, *Jerome Robbins' Broadway*
☆ Debbie Shapiro, *Jerome Robbins' Broadway*
Julie Wilson, *Legs Diamond*

DIRECTOR (PLAY)
Bill Irwin, *Largely New York*
Gregory Mosher, *Our Town*
Daniel Sullivan, *The Heidi Chronicles*
☆ Jerry Zaks, *Lend Me a Tenor*

DIRECTOR (MUSICAL)
Larry Carpenter, *Starmites*
☆ Jerome Robbins, *Jerome Robbins' Broadway*
Peter Mark Schifter, *Welcome to the Club*
Claudio Segovia and Hector Orezzoli, *Black and Blue*

BOOK (MUSICAL)
Category eliminated

SCORE
Category eliminated

SCENIC DESIGNER
☆ Santo Loquasto, *Café Crown*
Thomas Lynch, *The Heidi Chronicles*
Claudio Segovia and Hector Orezzoli, *Black and Blue*
Tony Walton, *Lend Me a Tenor*

COSTUME DESIGNER
Jane Greenwood, *Our Town*
Willa Kim, *Legs Diamond*
William Ivey Long, *Lend Me a Tenor*
☆ Claudio Segovia and Hector Orezzoli, *Black and Blue*

LIGHTING DESIGNER
Neil Peter Jampolis and Jane Reisman, *Black and Blue*
Brian Nason, *Metamorphosis*
Nancy Schertler, *Largely New York*
☆ Jennifer Tipton, *Jerome Robbins' Broadway*

CHOREOGRAPHER
Michele Assaf, *Starmites*
☆ Cholly Atkins, Henry Le Tang, Frankie Manning, and Fayard
    Nicholas, *Black and Blue*
Bill Irwin and Kimi Okada, *Largely New York*
Alan Johnson, *Legs Diamond*

REGIONAL THEATRE
☆ Hartford Stage Company, Hartford, Connecticut

The 1990s

"**I** just remember when I heard Sigourney Weaver announce my name as the winner—it was such a warm sound to my ears . . . as opposed to three other times I was nominated and lost, and the sound of another person's name (in that instance) was a harsh sound to my ears.

I was so happy for myself, my wife, who was one of the producers of 'Jelly's Last Jam', and my family and friends . . . and I was proud to walk up there and receive the Tony Award for all of us!"

Gregory Hines
Actor (Musical), *Jelly's Last Jam*

"I never dreamed of winning a Tony—I dreamed of being a part of the American Musical Theatre. So the 'win' for me was the chance to perform a great part in a great musical play. To then be rewarded with 'the prize' was an unexpected, delicious addition to an already amazing personal and professional journey. And the loving reaction from the crowd in the balcony was the best part of a memorable night. In retrospect, the honor is to be included on a list of talented performers that I have so long enjoyed and admired."

Tyne Daly
Actress (Musical), *Gypsy*

Photo: Anita and Steve Shevett

BEN VEREEN AND GREGORY HINES

1990

MUSICAL

Aspects of Love. Produced by The Really Useful Theatre Company, Inc.

☆ *City of Angels.* Produced by Nick Vanoff, Roger Berlind, Jujamcyn Theatres, Suntory International Corp., and The Shubert Organization.

Grand Hotel, The Musical. Produced by Martin Richards, Mary Lea Johnson, Sam Crothers, Sander Jacobs, Kenneth D. Greenblatt, Paramount Pictures, Jujamcyn Theatres, Patty Grubman, and Marvin A. Krauss.

Meet Me in St. Louis. Produced by Brickhill-Burke Productions, Christopher Seabrooke, and EPI Products.

PLAY

Lettice and Lovage by Peter Shaffer. Produced by The Shubert Organization, Robert Fox, Ltd., and Roger Berlind.

Prelude to a Kiss by Craig Lucas. Produced by Christopher Gould, Suzanne Golden, and Dodger Productions.

☆ *The Grapes of Wrath* by Frank Galati. Produced by The Shubert Organization, Steppenwolf Theatre Company, Suntory International Corp., and Jujamcyn Theatres.

The Piano Lesson by August Wilson. Produced by Lloyd Richards, Yale Repertory Theatre, Center Theatre Group/Ahmanson Theatre, Gordon Davidson, Jujamcyn Theatres, Benjamin Mordecai, in association with Eugene O'Neill Theatre Center, Huntington Theatre Company, Goodman Theatre, and Old Globe Theatre.

REVIVAL

☆ *Gypsy.* Produced by Barry and Fran Weissler, Kathy Levin, and Barry Brown.

Sweeney Todd. Produced by Circle in the Square Theatre, Theodore Mann, and Paul Libin.

The Circle. Produced by Elliot Martin, The Shubert Organization, and Suntory International Corp.

The Merchant of Venice. Produced by Duncan C. Weldon, Jerome Minskoff, Punch Productions, and Peter Hall.

LEADING ACTOR (PLAY)

Charles S. Dutton, *The Piano Lesson*

Dustin Hoffman, *The Merchant of Venice*

Tom Hulce, *A Few Good Men*

☆ Robert Morse, *Tru*

LEADING ACTRESS (PLAY)
Geraldine James, *The Merchant of Venice*
Mary-Louise Parker, *Prelude to a Kiss*
☆ Maggie Smith, *Lettice and Lovage*
Kathleen Turner, *Cat on a Hot Tin Roof*

FEATURED ACTOR (PLAY)
Rocky Carroll, *The Piano Lesson*
☆ Charles Durning, *Cat on a Hot Tin Roof*
Terry Kinney, *The Grapes of Wrath*
Gary Sinise, *The Grapes of Wrath*

FEATURED ACTRESS (PLAY)
Polly Holliday, *Cat on a Hot Tin Roof*
S. Epatha Merkerson, *The Piano Lesson*
Lois Smith, *The Grapes of Wrath*
☆ Margaret Tyzack, *Lettice and Lovage*

LEADING ACTOR (MUSICAL)
David Carroll, *Grand Hotel, The Musical*
Gregg Edelman, *City of Angels*
Bob Gunton, *Sweeney Todd*
☆ James Naughton, *City of Angels*

LEADING ACTRESS (MUSICAL)
Georgia Brown, *Threepenny Opera*
☆ Tyne Daly, *Gypsy*
Beth Fowler, *Sweeney Todd*
Liliane Montevecchi, *Grand Hotel, The Musical*

FEATURED ACTOR (MUSICAL)
René Auberjonois, *City of Angels*
Kevin Colson, *Aspects of Love*
Jonathan Hadary, *Gypsy*
☆ Michael Jeter, *Grand Hotel, The Musical*

FEATURED ACTRESS (MUSICAL)
☆ Randy Graff, *City of Angels*
Jane Krakowski, *Grand Hotel, The Musical*
Kathleen Rowe McAllen, *Aspects of Love*
Crista Moore, *Gypsy*

DIRECTOR (PLAY)
Michael Blakemore, *Lettice and Lovage*
☆ Frank Galati, *The Grapes of Wrath*

Peter Hall, *The Merchant of Venice*
Lloyd Richards, *The Piano Lesson*

DIRECTOR (MUSICAL)

Michael Blakemore, *City of Angels*
Trevor Nunn, *Aspects of Love*
Susan H. Schulman, *Sweeney Todd*
☆   Tommy Tune, *Grand Hotel, The Musical*

BOOK (MUSICAL)

Aspects of Love by Andrew Lloyd Webber
☆   *City of Angels* by Larry Gelbart
Grand Hotel, The Musical by Luther Davis
Meet Me in St. Louis by Hugh Wheeler

SCORE

Aspects of Love. Music by Andrew Lloyd Webber, lyrics by Don
     Black and Charles Hart.
☆   *City of Angels.* Music by Cy Coleman, lyrics by David Zippel.
Grand Hotel, The Musical. Music and lyrics by Robert Wright,
     George Forrest and Maury Yeston.
Meet Me in St. Louis. Music and lyrics by Hugh Martin and Ralph
     Blane.

SCENIC DESIGNER

Alexandra Byrne, *Some Americans Abroad*
Kevin Rigdon, *The Grapes of Wrath*
☆   Robin Wagner, *City of Angels*
Tony Walton, *Grand Hotel, The Musical*

COSTUME DESIGNER

Theoni V. Aldredge, *Gypsy*
Florence Klotz, *City of Angels*
☆   Santo Loquato, *Grand Hotel, The Musical*
Erin Quigley, *The Grapes of Wrath*

LIGHTING DESIGNER

☆   Jules Fisher, *Grand Hotel, The Musical*
Paul Gallo, *City of Angels*
Paul Pyant and Neil Peter Jampolis, *Orpheus Descending*
Kevin Rigdon, *The Grapes of Wrath*

CHOREOGRAPHER

Joan Brickhill, *Meet Me in St.Louis*
Graciela Daniele and Tina Paul, *Dangerous Games*
☆   Tommy Tune, *Grand Hotel, The Musical*

REGIONAL THEATRE
☆ Seattle Repertory Theatre

TONY HONOR
☆ Alfred Drake, for excellence in the theatre

1991

MUSICAL

Miss Saigon. Produced by Cameron Mackintosh.
Once on This Island. Produced by The Shubert Organization,
Capital Cities/ABC Inc., Suntory International, James
Walsh, and Playwrights Horizons.
The Secret Garden. Produced by Heidi Landesman, Rick Steiner,
Frederic H. Mayerson, Elizabeth Williams, Jujamcyn
Theaters, TV ASAHI, and Dodger Productions.
☆ *The Will Rogers Follies.* Produced by Pierre Cossette, Martin
Richards, Sam Crothers, James M. Nederlander, Stewart F.
Lane, Max Weitzenhoffer, and Japan Satellite
Broadcasting, Inc.

PLAY

☆ *Lost in Yonkers* by Neil Simon. Produced by Emanuel
Azenberg.
Our Country's Good by Timberlake Wertenbaker. Produced by
Frank and Woji Gero, Karl Sydow, Raymond L. Gaspard,
Frederick Zollo, Diana Bliss, and Hartford Stage Company.
Shadowlands by William Nicholson. Produced by Elliot Martin,
James M. Nederlander, Brian Eastman, Terry Allen
Kramer, and Roger L. Stevens.
Six Degrees of Separation by John Guare. Produced by Lincoln
Center Theater, Gregory Mosher, and Bernard Gersten.

REVIVAL

☆ *Fiddler on the Roof.* Produced by Barry and Fran Weissler and
Pace Theatrical Group.
The Miser. Produced by Circle in the Square Theatre, Theodore
Mann, and Paul Libin.
Peter Pan. Produced by James M. Nederlander, Arthur Rubin,
Thomas P. McCoy, Keith Stava, P.P. Investments, Inc., and
Jon B. Platt.

LEADING ACTOR (PLAY)

Peter Frechette, *Our Country's Good*

☆ Nigel Hawthorne, *Shadowlands*
Tom McGowan, *La Bête*
Courtney B. Vance, *Six Degrees of Separation*

LEADING ACTRESS (PLAY)
Stockard Channing, *Six Degrees of Separation*
Julie Harris, *Lucifer's Child*
Cherry Jones, *Our Country's Good*
☆ Mercedes Ruehl, *Lost in Yonkers*

FEATURED ACTOR (PLAY)
Adam Arkin, *I Hate Hamlet*
Dylan Baker, *La Bête*
Stephen Lang, *The Speed of Darkness*
☆ Kevin Spacey, *Lost in Yonkers*

FEATURED ACTRESS (PLAY)
Amelia Campbell, *Our Country's Good*
Kathryn Erbe, *The Speed of Darkness*
J. Smith-Cameron, *Our Country's Good*
☆ Irene Worth, *Lost in Yonkers*

LEADING ACTOR (MUSICAL)
Keith Carradine, *The Will Rogers Follies*
Paul Hipp, *Buddy*
☆ Jonathan Pryce, *Miss Saigon*
Topol, *Fiddler on the Roof*

LEADING ACTRESS (MUSICAL)
June Angela, *Shogun: The Musical*
Dee Hoty, *The Will Rogers Follies*
Cathy Rigby, *Peter Pan*
☆ Lea Salonga, *Miss Saigon*

FEATURED ACTOR (MUSICAL)
Bruce Adler, *Those Were the Days*
☆ Hinton Battle, *Miss Saigon*
Gregg Burge, *Oh, Kay!*
Willy Falk, *Miss Saigon*

FEATURED ACTRESS (MUSICAL)
☆ Daisy Eagan, *The Secret Garden*
Alison Fraser, *The Secret Garden*
Cady Huffman, *The Will Rogers Follies*
La Chanze, *Once on This Island*

DIRECTOR (PLAY)
Richard Jones, *La Bête*
Mark Lamos, *Our Country's Good*
Gene Saks, *Lost in Yonkers*
☆ Jerry Zaks, *Six Degrees of Separation*

DIRECTOR (MUSICAL)
Graciela Daniele, *Once on This Island*
Nicholas Hytner, *Miss Saigon*
Eleanor Reissa, *Those Were the Days*
☆ Tommy Tune, *The Will Rogers Follies*

BOOK (MUSICAL)
Miss Saigon by Alain Boublil and Claude-Michel Schönberg
Once on This Island by Lynn Ahrens
☆ *The Secret Garden* by Marsha Norman
The Will Rogers Follies by Peter Stone

SCORE (MUSICAL)
Miss Saigon. Music by Claude-Michel Schönberg, lyrics by Richard Maltby, Jr. and Alain Boublil.
Once on This Island. Music by Stephen Flaherty, lyrics by Lynn Ahrens.
The Secret Garden. Music by Lucy Simon, lyrics by Marsha Norman.
☆ *The Will Rogers Follies*. Music by Cy Coleman, lyrics by Betty Comden and Adolph Green.

SCENIC DESIGNER
Richard Hudson, *La Bête*
☆ Heidi Landesman, *The Secret Garden*
John Napier, *Miss Saigon*
Tony Walton, *The Will Rogers Follies*

COSTUME DESIGNER
Theoni V. Aldredge, *The Secret Garden*
Judy Deering, *Once on This Island*
☆ Willa Kim, *The Will Rogers Follies*
Patricia Zipprodt, *Shogun: The Musical*

LIGHTING DESIGNER
☆ Jules Fisher, *The Will Rogers Follies*
David Hershey, *Miss Saigon*
Allen Lee Hughes, *Once on This Island*
Jennifer Tipton, *La Bête*

CHOREOGRAPHER
Bob Avian, *Miss Saigon*
Graciela Daniele, *Once on This Island*
Dan Siretta, *Oh, Kay!*
☆ Tommy Tune, *The Will Rogers Follies*

REGIONAL THEATRE
☆ Yale Repertory Theater, New Haven, Connecticut

TONY HONOR
☆ Father George Moore (posthumous)

1992

MUSICAL
☆ *Crazy for You.* Produced by Rodger Horchow and Elizabeth
Williams.
Falsettos. Produced by Barry and Fran Weissler.
Five Guys Named Moe. Produced by Cameron Mackintosh.
Jelly's Last Jam. Produced by Margo Lion, Pamela Koslow,
PolyGram Diversified Entertainment, 126 Second Avenue
Corp./Hal Luftig, Roger Hess, Jujamcyn Theaters/TV Asahi,
and Herb Alpert.

PLAY
☆ *Dancing at Lughnasa* by Brian Friel. Produced by Noel
Pearson, Bill Kenwright, and Joseph Harris.
Four Baboons Adoring the Sun by John Guare. Produced by Lincoln
Center Theater, André Bishop, and Bernard Gersten.
Two Shakespearean Actors by Richard Nelson. Produced by Lincoln
Center Theater, Gregory Mosher, and Bernard Gersten.
Two Trains Running by August Wilson. Produced by Lloyd
Richard's Yale Repertory Theatre, Stan Wojewodski, Jr.,
Center Theatre Group/Ahmanson Theatre, Gordon
Davidson, Jujamcyn Theaters, Benjamin Mordecai,
Huntington Theatre Company, Seattle Repertory Theatre,
and Old Globe Theatre.

REVIVAL
☆ *Guys and Dolls.* Produced by Dodger Productions, Roger
Berlind, Jujamcyn Theatres/TV Asahi, Kardana
Productions, and The John F. Kennedy Center for the
Performing Arts.
The Most Happy Fella. Produced by The Goodspeed Opera House,
Center Theatre Group/Ahmanson Theatre, Lincoln Center

Theater, The Shubert Organization, and Japan Satellite Broadcasting/Stagevision, Suntory International Corporation.

On Borrowed Time. Produced by Circle in the Square Theatre, Theodore Mann, Robert Buckley, and Paul Libin.

The Visit. Produced by Roundabout Theatre Company, Todd Haimes, and Gene Feist.

LEADING ACTOR (PLAY)

Alan Alda, *Jake's Women*
Alec Baldwin, *A Streetcar Named Desire*
Brian Bedford, *Two Shakespearean Actors*
☆ Judd Hirsch, *Conversations with My Father*

LEADING ACTRESS (PLAY)

Jane Alexander, *The Visit*
Stockard Channing, *Four Baboons Adoring the Sun*
☆ Glenn Close, *Death and the Maiden*
Judith Ivey, *Park Your Car in Harvard Yard*

FEATURED ACTOR (PLAY)

Roscoe Lee Browne, *Two Trains Running*
☆ Larry Fishburne, *Two Trains Running*
Zeljko Ivanek, *Two Shakespearean Actors*
Tony Shalhoub, *Conversations with My Father*

FEATURED ACTRESS (PLAY)

☆ Brid Brennan, *Dancing at Lughnasa*
Rosaleen Linehan, *Dancing at Lughnasa*
Cynthia Martells, *Two Trains Running*
Dearbhia Molly, *Dancing at Lughnasa*

LEADING ACTOR (MUSICAL)

Harry Groener, *Crazy for You*
☆ Gregory Hines, *Jelly's Last Jam*
Nathan Lane, *Guys and Dolls*
Michael Rupert, *Falsettos*

LEADING ACTRESS (MUSICAL)

Jodi Benson, *Crazy for You*
Josie de Guzman, *Guys and Dolls*
Sophie Hayden, *The Most Happy Fella*
☆ Faith Prince, *Guys and Dolls*

FEATURED ACTOR (MUSICAL)

Bruce Adler, *Crazy for You*
Keith David, *Jelly's Last Jam*

Jonathan Kaplan, *Falsettos*
☆ Scott Waara, *The Most Happy Fella*

FEATURED ACTRESS (MUSICAL)

Liz Larsen, *The Most Happy Fella*
☆ Tonya Pinkins, *Jelly's Last Jam*
Vivian Reed, *The High Rollers Social & Pleasure Club*
Barbara Walsh, *Falsettos*

DIRECTOR (PLAY)

Peter Hall, *Four Baboons Adoring the Sun*
☆ Patrick Mason, *Dancing at Lughnasa*
Jack O'Brien, *Two Shakespearean Actors*
Daniel Sullivan, *Conversations with My Father*

DIRECTOR (MUSICAL)

James Lapine, *Falsettos*
Mike Ockrent, *Crazy for You*
George C. Wolfe, *Jelly's Last Jam*
☆ Jerry Zaks, *Guys and Dolls*

BOOK (MUSICAL)

Crazy for You by Ken Ludwig
☆ *Falsettos* by William Finn and James Lapine
Five Guys Named Moe by Clarke Peters
Jelly's Last Jam by George C. Wolfe

SCORE (MUSICAL)

☆ *Falsettos*. Music and lyrics by William Finn.
Jelly's Last Jam. Music by Ferdinand Le Menthe "Jelly Roll" Morton
    and Luther Henderson, lyrics by Susan Birkenhead.
Metro. Music by Januez Stoklosa, lyrics by Agata and Maryna
    Miklaszewska and Mary Bracken Philips.
Nick & Nora. Music by Charles Strouse, lyrics by Richard Maltby, Jr.

SCENIC DESIGNER

John Lee Beatty, *A Small Family Business*
Joe Vanek, *Dancing at Lughnasa*
Robin Wagner, *Jelly's Last Jam*
☆ Tony Walton, *Guys and Dolls*

COSTUME DESIGNER

Jane Greenwood, *Two Shakespearean Actors*
Toni-Leslie James, *Jelly's Last Jam*
☆ William Ivey Long, *Crazy for You*
Joe Vanek, *Dancing at Lughnasa*

LIGHTING DESIGNER
☆ Jules Fisher, *Jelly's Last Jam*
Paul Gallo, *Crazy for You*
Paul Gallo, *Guys and Dolls*
Richard Pilbrow, *Four Baboons Adoring the Sun*

CHOREOGRAPHER
Terry John Bates, *Dancing at Lughnasa*
Christopher Chadman, *Guys and Dolls*
Hope Clarke, Gregory Hines, Ted L. Levy, *Jelly's Last Jam*
☆ Susan Stroman, *Crazy for You*

REGIONAL THEATRE
☆ The Goodman Theatre, Chicago, Illinois

TONY HONOR
☆ *The Fantasticks*

1993

MUSICAL
Blood Brothers. Produced by Bill Kenwright.
The Goodbye Girl. Produced by Office Two-One Inc., Gladys
    Nederlander, Stewart F. Lane, James M. Nederlander,
    Richard Kagan, and Emanuel Azenberg.
☆ *Kiss of the Spider Woman—The Musical.* Produced by The Live
    Entertainment Corp. of Canada/Garth Drabinsky.
The Who's Tommy. Produced by PACE Theatrical Group, Dodger
    Productions, and Kardana Productions, Inc.

PLAY
☆ *Angels in American: Millennium Approaches* by Tony Kushner.
    Produced by Jujamcyn Theatres, Mark Taper
    Forum/Gordon Davidson, Margo Lion, Susan Quint Gallin,
    Jon B. Platt, The Baruch-Frankel-Viertel Group, Frederick
    Zollo, and Herb Alpert.
The Sisters Rosensweig by Wendy Wasserstein. Produced by Lincoln
    Center Theater, André Bishop, and Bernard Gersten.
Someone Who'll Watch Over Me by Frank McGuinness. Produced by
    Noel Pearson, The Shubert Organization, and Joseph
    Harris.
The Song of Jacob Zulu by Tug Yourgrau. Produced by Steppenwolf
    Theatre Company, Randall Arney, Stephen Eich, Albert
    Poland, Susan Liederman, Bette Cerf Hill, and Maurice
    Rosenfield.

REVIVAL
☆ *Anna Christie.* Produced by Roundabout Theatre Company and Todd Haimes.
Saint Joan. Produced by National Actors Theatre, Tony Randall, and Duncan C. Weldon.
The Price. Produced by Roundabout Theatre Company and Todd Haimes.
Wilder, Wilder, Wilder. Produced by Circle in the Square Theatre, Theodore Mann, George Elmer, Paul Libin, Willow Cabin Theatre Company, Edward Berkeley, Adam Oliensis, and Maria Radman.

LEADING ACTOR (PLAY)
K. Todd Freeman, *The Song of Jacob Zulu*
☆ Ron Leibman, *Angels in America: Millennium Approaches*
Liam Neeson, *Anna Christie*
Stephen Rea, *Someone Who'll Watch Over Me*

LEADING ACTRESS (PLAY)
Jane Alexander, *The Sisters Rosensweig*
☆ Madeline Kahn, *The Sisters Rosensweig*
Lynn Redgrave, *Shakespeare for My Father*
Natasha Richardson, *Anna Christie*

FEATURED ACTOR (PLAY)
Robert Sean Leonard, *Candida*
Joe Mantello, *Angels in America: Millennium Approaches*
Zakes Mokae, *The Song of Jacob Zulu*
☆ Stephen Spinella, *Angels in America: Millennium Approaches*

FEATURED ACTRESS (PLAY)
Kathleen Chalfant, *Angels in America: Millennium Approaches*
Marcia Gay Harden, *Angels in America: Millennium Approaches*
Anne Meara, *Anna Christie*
☆ Debra Monk, *Redwood Curtain*

LEADING ACTOR (MUSICAL)
☆ Brent Carver, *Kiss of the Spider Woman—The Musical*
Tim Curry, *My Favorite Year*
Con O'Neill, *Blood Brothers*
Martin Short, *The Goodbye Girl*

LEADING ACTRESS (MUSICAL)
Ann Crumb, *Anna Karenina*
Stephanie Lawrence, *Blood Brothers*
Bernadette Peters, *The Goodbye Girl*

☆ Chita Rivera, Kiss of the Spider Woman—The Musical

FEATURED ACTOR (MUSICAL)

Michael Cerveris, The Who's Tommy
☆ Anthony Crivello, Kiss of the Spider Woman—The Musical
Gregg Edelman, Anna Karenina
Paul Kandel, The Who's Tommy

FEATURED ACTRESS (MUSICAL)

Jan Graveson, Blood Brothers
Lainie Kazan, My Favorite Year
☆ Andrea Martin, My Favorite Year
Marcia Mitzman, The Who's Tommy

DIRECTOR (PLAY)

David Leveaux, Anna Christie
Eric Simonson, The Song of Jacob Zulu
Daniel Sullivan, The Sisters Rosensweig
☆ George C. Wolfe, Angels in America: Millennium Approaches

DIRECTOR (MUSICAL)

Bill Kenwright and Bob Thomson, Blood Brothers
Michael Kidd, The Goodbye Girl
☆ Des McAnuff, The Who's Tommy
Harold Prince, Kiss of the Spider Woman—The Musical

BOOK (MUSICAL)

Anna Karenina by Peter Kellogg
Blood Brothers by Willy Russell
☆ Kiss of the Spider Woman—The Musical by Terrence McNally
The Who's Tommy by Pete Townsend and Des McAnuff

SCORE (MUSICAL)

Anna Karenina. Music by Daniel Levine, lyrics by Peter Kellogg.
☆ Kiss of the Spider Woman—The Musical. Music by John Kander,
    lyrics by Fred Ebb.
The Song of Jacob Zulu. Music by Ladysmith Black Mambazo, lyrics
    by Tug Yourgrau and Ladysmith Black Mambazo.
☆ The Who's Tommy. Music and lyrics by Pete Townshend.

SCENIC DESIGNER

☆ John Arnone, The Who's Tommy
John Lee Beatty, Redwood Curtain
Jerome Sirlin, Kiss of the Spider Woman—The Musical
Robin Wagner, Angels in America: Millennium Approaches

COSTUME DESIGNER
Jane Greenwood, *The Sisters Rosensweig*
☆ Florence Klotz, *Kiss of the Spider Woman—The Musical*
Erin Quigley, *The Song of Jacob Zulu*
David C. Woolard, *The Who's Tommy*

LIGHTING DESIGNER
Howell Binkley, *Kiss of the Spider Woman—The Musical*
Jules Fisher, *Angels in America: Millennium Approaches*
Dennis Parichy, *Redwood Curtain*
☆ Chris Parry, *The Who's Tommy*

CHOREOGRAPHER
☆ Wayne Cilento, *The Who's Tommy*
Graciela Daniele, *The Goodbye Girl*
Vincent Patterson and Rob Marshall, *Kiss of the Spider Woman—The Musical*
Randy Skinner, *Ain't Broadway Grand*

REGIONAL THEATRE
☆ La Jolla Playhouse, La Jolla, California

SPECIAL AWARDS
☆ *Oklahoma!*—50th Anniversary

TONY HONORS
☆ IATSE
☆ Broadway Cares / Equity Fights AIDS

1994

MUSICAL
A Grand Night for Singing. Produced by Roundabout Theatre Company, Todd Haimes, Gregory Dawson, and Steve Paul.
Disney's *Beauty and the Beast.* Produced by Walt Disney Theatrical Productions/Robert McTyre and Ron Logan.
Cyrano: The Musical. Produced by Joop van den Ende in association with Peter T. Kulok.
☆ *Passion.* Produced by The Shubert Organization, Capital Cities/ABC, Roger Berlind, Scott Rudin, and Lincoln Center Theater.

PLAY
☆ *Angels in America: Perestroika* by Tony Kushner. Produced by Jujamcyn Theatres and The Mark Taper Forum/Gordon

Davidson, Artistic Director with Margo Lion, Susan Quint
Gallin, John B. Platt, The Baruch-Frankel-Viertel Group,
and Frederick Zollo in association with the New York
Shakespeare Festival, Mordecai/Cole Productions, and
Herb Alpert.
Broken Glass by Arthur Miller. Produced by Robert
Whitehead/Roger L. Stevens/Lars Schmidt, Spring Sirkin,
Terri and Timothy Childs, and Herb Alpert.
The Kentucky Cycle by Robert Schenkkan. Produced by David
Richenthal, Gene R. Korf, Roger L. Stevens, Jennifer
Manocherian, Annette Niemtzow, Mark Taper
Forum/Intiman Theatre Company, and The John F.
Kennedy Center for the Performing Arts in association
with Benjamin Mordecai.
Twilight: Los Angeles, 1992 by Anna Deavere Smith. Produced by
Benjamin Mordecai, Laura Rafaty, Ric Wanetik, The New
York Shakespeare Festival, Mark Taper Forum, Harriett
Newman Leve, Jeanne Rizzo, James D. Stern, Daryl Roth,
Jo-Lynne Worley, Ronald A. Pizzuti, The Booking Office,
Inc., and Freddy Bienstock.

REVIVAL (PLAY)

Abe Lincoln in Illinois. Produced by Lincoln Center Theater, André
Bishop and Bernard Gersten.
☆　*An Inspector Calls.* Produced by Noel Pearson, The Shubert
Organization, Capital Cities/ABC, and Joseph Harris.
Medea. Produced by Bill Kenwright.
Timon of Athens. Produced by National Actors Theatre and Tony
Randall.

REVIVAL (MUSICAL)

☆　*Carousel.* Produced by Lincoln Center Theater, André Bishop,
Bernard Gersten, The Royal National Theatre, Cameron
Mackintosh, and The Rodgers & Hammerstein Organization.
Damn Yankees. Produced by Mitchell Maxwell, PolyGram
Diversified Entertainment, Dan Markley, Kevin McCollum,
Victoria Maxwell, Fred H. Krones, Andrea Nasher, The
Frankel-Viertel-Baruch Group, Paula Heil Fisher, Julie
Ross, Jon B. Platt, Alan Schuster, and Peter Breger.
Grease. Produced by Barry and Fran Weissler and Jujamcyn
Theatres.
She Loves Me. Produced by Roundabot Theatre Company, Todd
Haimes, James M. Nederlander, Elliot Martin, Herbert
Wasserman, Freddy Bienstock, and Roger L. Stevens.

LEADING ACTOR (PLAY)
Brian Bedford, *Timon of Athens*
Christopher Plummer, *No Man's Land*
☆ Stephen Spinella, *Angels in America: Perestroika*
Sam Waterston, *Abe Lincoln in Illinois*

LEADING ACTRESS (PLAY)
Nancy Marchand, *Black Comedy*
☆ Diana Rigg, *Medea*
Joan Rivers, *Sally Marr . . . and Her Escorts*
Anna Deavere Smith, *Twilight: Los Angeles, 1992*

FEATURED ACTOR (PLAY)
Larry Bryggman, *Picnic*
David Marshall Grant, *Angels in America: Perestroika*
Gary Itzin, *The Kentucky Cycle*
☆ Jeffrey Wright, *Angels in America: Perestroika*

FEATURED ACTRESS (PLAY)
☆ Jane Adams, *An Inspector Calls*
Debra Monk, *Picnic*
Jeanne Paulsen, *The Kentucky Cycle*
Anne Pitoniak, *Picnic*

LEADING ACTOR (MUSICAL)
☆ Boyd Gaines, *She Loves Me*
Victor Garber, *Damn Yankees*
Terrence Mann, *Disney's Beauty and the Beast*
Jere Shea, *Passion*

LEADING ACTRESS (MUSICAL)
Susan Egan, *Disney's Beauty and the Beast*
Dee Hoty, *The Best Little Whorehouse Goes Public*
Judy Kuhn, *She Loves Me*
☆ Donna Murphy, *Passion*

FEATURED ACTOR (MUSICAL)
Tom Aldredge, *Passion*
Gary Beach, *Disney's Beauty and the Beast*
☆ Jarrod Emick, *Damn Yankees*
Jonathan Freeman, *She Loves Me*

FEATURED ACTOR (MUSICAL)
Marcia Lewis, *Grease*
Sally Mayes, *She Loves Me*
Marin Mazzie, *Passion*

AUDRA MCDONALD

☆ Audra Ann McDonald, *Carousel*

DIRECTOR (PLAY)
☆ Stephen Daldry, An Inspector Calls
Gerald Gutierrez, Abe Lincoln in Illinois
Michael Langham, Timon of Athens
George C. Wolfe, Angels in America: Perestroika

DIRECTOR (MUSICAL)
Scott Ellis, She Loves Me
☆ Nicholas Hytner, Carousel

James Lapine, *Passion*
Robert Jess Roth, Disney's *Beauty and the Beast*

Book (Musical)
A Grand Night for Singing by Walter Bobbie
Disney's *Beauty and the Beast* by Linda Woolverton
Cyrano: The Musical by Koen van Dijk
☆ *Passion* by James Lapine

Score
Disney's *Beauty and the Beast*. Music by Alan Menken, lyrics by
 Howard Ashman and Tim Rice.
Cyrano: The Musical. Music by Ad van Dijk, lyrics by Koen van
 Dijk, Peter Reeves, and Sheldon Harnick.
☆ *Passion*. Music and lyrics by Stephen Sondheim.

Scenic Designer
☆ Bob Crowley, *Carousel*
Peter J. Davison, *Medea*
Ian MacNeil, *An Inspector Calls*
Tony Walton, *She Loves Me*

Costume Designer
David Charles and Jane Greenwood, *She Loves Me*
Jane Greenwood, *Passion*
☆ Ann Hould-Ward, Disney's *Beauty and the Beast*
Yan Tax, *Cyrano: The Musical*

Lighting Designer
Beverly Emmons, *Passion*
Jules Fisher, *Angels in America: Perestroika*
☆ Rick Fisher, *An Inspector Calls*
Natasha Katz, Disney's *Beauty and the Beast*

Choreographer
Jeff Calhoun, *Grease*
☆ Sir Kenneth MacMillan, *Carousel*
Rob Marshall, *Damn Yankees*
Rob Marshall, *She Loves Me*

Regional Theatre
☆ McCarter Theatre Center for the Performing Arts, Princeton,
 New Jersey

Special Award
☆ Lifetime Achievement: Jessica Tandy and Hume Cronyn

1995

MUSICAL

Smokey Joe's Cafe. Produced by Richard Frankel, Thomas Viertel, Steven Baruch, Jujamcyn Theaters/Jack Viertel, Rick Steiner, Frederic H. Mayerson, and Center Theatre Group/Ahmanson Theatre/Gordon Davidson.
☆   *Sunset Boulevard.* Produced by The Really Useful Company, Inc.

PLAY

Arcadia by Tom Stoppard. Produced by Lincoln Center Theatre, André Bishop, and Bernard Gersten.
Having Our Say by Emily Mann. Produced by Camille O. Cosby and Judith Rutherford James.
Indiscretions by Jean Cocteau. Produced by The Shubert Organization, Roger Berlind, Capital Cities/ABS, and Scott Rudin.
☆   *Love! Valour! Compassion!* by Terrence McNally. Produced by Manhattan Theatre Club, Lynne Meadow, Barry Grove, and Jujamcyn Theaters.

REVIVAL (PLAY)

Hamlet. Produced by Dodger Productions, Roger Berlind, Endemol Theatre Productions, Inc., Jujamcyn Theaters, Kardana Productions, Inc., Scott Rudin, and The Almeida Theatre Company.
☆   *The Heiress.* Produced by Lincoln Center Theatre, André Bishop, and Bernard Gersten.
The Molière Comedies. Produced by Roundabout Theatre Company and Todd Haimes.
The Rose Tattoo. Produced by Circle in the Square Theatre, Theodore Mann, Josephine R. Abady, and Robert Bennett.

REVIVAL (MUSICAL)

How to Succeed in Business Without Really Trying. Produced by Dodger Productions & Kardana Productions, Inc., The John F. Kennedy Center for the Performing Arts, and The Nederlander Organization.
☆   *Show Boat.* Produced by Livent (U.S.) Inc.

LEADING ACTOR (PLAY)

Brian Bedford, *The Molière Comedies*
☆   Ralph Fiennes, *Hamlet*
Roger Rees, *Indiscretions*
Joe Sears, *A Tuna Christmas*

LEADING ACTRESS (PLAY)
Mary Alice, *Having Our Say*
Eileen Atkins, *Indiscretions*
☆ Cherry Jones, *The Heiress*
Helen Mirren, *A Month in the Country*

FEATURED ACTOR (PLAY)
Stephen Bogardus, *Love! Valour! Compassion!*
☆ John Glover, *Love! Valour! Compassion!*
Anthony Heald, *Love! Valour! Compassion!*
Jude Law, *Indiscretions*

FEATURED ACTRESS (PLAY)
Suzanne Bertish, *The Molière Comedies*
Cynthia Nixon, *Indiscretions*
Mercedes Ruehl, *The Shadow Box*
☆ Frances Sternhagen, *The Heiress*

LEADING ACTOR (MUSICAL)
☆ Matthew Broderick, *How to Succeed in Business Without Really Trying*
Alan Campbell, *Sunset Boulevard*
Mark Jacoby, *Show Boat*
John McMartin, *Show Boat*

LEADING ACTRESS (MUSICAL)
☆ Glenn Close, *Sunset Boulevard*
Rebecca Luker, *Show Boat*

FEATURED ACTOR (MUSICAL)
Michel Bell, *Show Boat*
Joel Blum, *Show Boat*
Victor Trent Cook, *Smokey Joe's Café*
☆ George Hearn, *Sunset Boulevard*

FEATURED ACTRESS (MUSICAL)
☆ Greta Boston, *Show Boat*
Brenda Braxton, *Smokey Joe's Café*
B. J. Crosby, *Smokey Joe's Café*
DeLee Lively, *Smokey Joe's Café*

DIRECTOR (PLAY)
Gerald Gutierrez, *The Heiress*
Emily Mann, *Having Our Say*
☆ Joe Mantello, *Love! Valour! Compassion!*
Sean Mathias, *Indiscretions*

DIRECTOR (MUSICAL)

Des McAnuff, *How to Succeed in Business Without Really Trying*
Trevor Nunn, *Sunset Boulevard*
☆ Harold S. Prince, *Show Boat*
Jerry Zaks, *Smokey Joe's Cafe*

BOOK (MUSICAL)

☆ *Sunset Boulevard* by Don Black and Christopher Hampton

SCORE

☆ *Sunset Boulevard*. Music and lyrics by Andrew Lloyd Webber, Don Black, and Christopher Hampton.

SCENIC DESIGN

John Lee Beatty, *The Heiress*
Stephen Brimson Lewis, *Indiscretions*
☆ John Napier, *Sunset Boulevard*
Mark Thompson, *Arcadia*

COSTUME DESIGN

Jane Greenwood, *The Heiress*
☆ Florence Klotz, *Show Boat*
Stephen Lewis, *Indiscretions*
Anthony Powell, *Sunset Boulevard*

LIGHTING DESIGNER

☆ Andrew Bridge, *Sunset Boulevard*
Beverly Emmons, *The Heiress*
Mark Henderson, *Indiscretions*
Paul Pyant, *Arcadia*

CHOREOGRAPHY

Bob Avian, *Sunset Boulevard*
Wayne Cilento, *How to Succeed in Business Without Really Trying*
Joey McKneely, *Smokey Joe's Café*
☆ Susan Stroman, *Show Boat*

REGIONAL THEATRE

☆ Goodspeed Opera House

SPECIAL AWARD

☆ Lifetime Achievement: Carol Channing
☆ Lifetime Achievement: Harvey Sabinson

TONY HONOR

☆ National Endowment for the Arts, Jane Alexander, Chairman

1996

MUSICAL

Bring in 'da Noise, Bring in 'da Funk. Produced by The Joseph Papp Public Theatre/New York Shakespeare Festival, George C. Wolfe, and Joey Parnes.

Chronicle of a Death Foretold. Produced by Lincoln Center Theatre, André Bishop, Bernard Gersten, and INTAR Hispanic Arts Center.

☆ *Rent*. Produced by Jeffrey Seller, Kevin McCollum, Allan S. Gordon, and The New York Theatre Workshop.

Swinging on a Star. Produced by Richard Seader, Mary Burke Kramer, Paul B. Berkowsky, and Angels of the Arts.

PLAY

Buried Child by Sam Shepard. Produced by Frederick Zollo, Nicholas Paleologos, Jane Harmon, Nina Keanneally, Gary Sinise, Edwin Schloss, and Liz Oliver.

☆ *Master Class* by Terrence McNally. Produced by Robert Whitehead, Lewis Allen, and Spring Sirkin.

Racing Demon by David Hare. Produced by Lincoln Center Theatre, André Bishop, and Bernard Gersten.

Seven Guitars by August Wilson. Produced by Sageworks, Benjamin Mordecai, Center Theatre Group/Ahmanson Theatre, Gordon Davidson, Herb Alpert/Margo Lion, Scott Rudin/Paramount Pictures, Jujamcyn Theaters, Goodman Theatre, Huntington Theatre Company, American Conservatory Theatre, and Manhattan Theatre Club.

REVIVAL (PLAY)

☆ A *Delicate Balance*. Produced by Lincoln Center Theatre, André Bishop, and Bernard Gersten.

A *Midsummer Night's Dream*. Produced by Terry Allen Kramer, James L. Nederlander, Carole Shorenstein Hays, The John F. Kennedy Center for the Performing Arts, Elizabeth Ireland McCann, and The Royal Shakespeare Company.

An Ideal Husband. Produced by Bill Kenwright.

Inherit the Wind. Produced by National Actors Theatre and Tony Randall.

REVIVAL (MUSICAL)

A *Funny Thing Happened on the Way to the Forum*. Produced by Jujamcyn Theaters, Scott Rudin/Paramount Pictures, The Viertel-Baruch-Frankel Group, Roger Berlind, and Dodger Productions.

Company. Produced by Roundabout Theatre Company, Todd Haimes, and Ellen Richard.

Hello, Dolly. Produced by Manny Kladitis, Magic Productions and Theatricals, Pace Theatrical Group, Inc., and Jon B. Platt.

☆ *The King and I.* Produced by Dodger Productions, The John F. Kennedy Center for the Performing Arts, James M. Nederlander, Perseus Productions, John Frost, The Adelaide Festival Centre, and The Rodgers and Hammerstein Organization.

LEADING ACTOR (PLAY)
Philip Bosco, *Moon Over Buffalo*
☆ George Grizzard, *A Delicate Balance*
George C. Scott, *Inherit the Wind*
Martin Shaw, *An Ideal Husband*

LEADING ACTRESS (PLAY)
Carol Burnett, *Moon Over Buffalo*
☆ Zoe Caldwell, *Master Class*
Rosemary Harris, *A Delicate Balance*
Elaine Stritch, *A Delicate Balance*

FEATURED ACTOR (PLAY)
James Gammon, *Buried Child*
Roger Robinson, *Seven Guitars*
Reg Rogers, *Holiday*
☆ Ruben Santiago-Hudson, *Seven Guitars*

FEATURED ACTRESS (PLAY)
Viola Davis, *Seven Guitars*
☆ Audra McDonald, *Master Class*
Michele Shay, *Seven Guitars*
Lois Smith, *Buried Child*

LEADING ACTOR (MUSICAL)
Savion Glover, *Bring in 'da Noise, Bring in 'da Funk*
☆ Nathan Lane, *A Funny Thing Happened on the Way to the Forum*
Adam Pascal, *Rent*
Lou Diamond Phillips, *The King and* I

LEADING ACTRESS (MUSICAL)
Julie Andrews, *Victoria/Victoria*
Crista Moore, *Big*
☆ Donna Murphy, *The King and* I
Daphne Rubin-Vega, *Rent*

FEATURED ACTOR (MUSICAL)
☆ Wilson Jermaine Heredia, *Rent*
Lewis J. Stadlen, A *Funny Thing Happened on the Way to the Forum*
Brett Tabisel, *Big*
Scott Wise, *State Fair*

FEATURED ACTRESS (MUSICAL)
Joohee Choi, *The King and* I
Veanne Cox, *Company*
☆ Ann Duquesnay, *Bring in 'da Noise, Bring in 'da Funk*
Idina Menzel, *Rent*

DIRECTOR (PLAY)
☆ Gerald Gutierrez, A *Delicate Balance*
Peter Hall, An *Ideal Husband*
Lloyd Richards, *Seven Guitars*
Gary Sinise, *Buried Child*

DIRECTOR (MUSICAL)
Michael Greif, *Rent*
Christopher Renshaw, *The King and* I
☆ George C. Wolfe, *Bring in 'da Noise, Bring in 'da Funk*
Jerry Zaks, A *Funny Thing Happened on the Way to the Forum*

BOOK (MUSICAL)
John Weidman, *Big*
Reg E. Gaines, *Bring in 'da Noise, Bring in 'da Funk*
Graciela Daniele, Jim Lewis, Michael John LaChiusa, *Chronicle of a Death Foretold*
☆ Jonathan Larson, *Rent*

SCORE
Big. Music by David Shire, lyrics by Richard Maltby, Jr.
Bring in 'da Noise, Bring in 'da Funk. Music by Daryl Waters, Zane Mark, and Ann Duquesnay, lyrics by Reg E. Gaines and George C. Wolfe.
☆ *Rent*. Music and lyrics by Jonathan Larson.
State Fair. Music by Richard Rodgers, lyrics by Oscar Hammerstein II.

SCENIC DESIGNER
John Lee Beatty, A *Delicate Balance*
Scott Bradley, *Seven Guitars*
☆ Brian Thomson, *The King and* I
Anthony Ward, A *Midsummer Night's Dream*

COSTUME DESIGNER
Jane Greenwood, A *Delicate Balance*
☆   Roger Kirk, *The King and* I
Allison Reeds, *Buried Child*
Paul Tazewell, *Bring in 'da Noise, Bring in 'da Funk*

LIGHTING DESIGNER
Christopher Akerlind, *Seven Guitars*
Blake Burba, *Rent*
☆   Jules Fisher and Peggy Eisenhauer, *Bring in 'da Noise, Bring in 'da Funk*
Nigel Levings, *The King and* I

CHOREOGRAPHER
Graciela Daniele, *Chronicle of a Death Foretold*
☆   Savion Glover, *Bring in 'da Noise, Bring in 'da Funk*
Susan Stroman, *Big*
Marlies Yearby, *Rent*

REGIONAL THEATRE
☆   The Alley Theatre, Houston, Texas

1997

MUSICAL
Juan Darién, A Carnival Mass. Produced by Lincoln Center Theatre, André Bishop, Bernard Gersten, and Music-Theatre Group.
Steel Pier. Produced by Roger Berlind.
The Life. Produced by Roger Berlind, Martin Richards, Cy Coleman, and Sam Crothers.
☆   *Titanic*. Produced by Dodger Endemol Theatricals, Richard S. Pechter, and The John F. Kennedy Center for the Performing Arts.

PLAY
Skylight by David Hare. Produced by Robert Fox, Roger Berlind, Joan Cullman, Scott Rudin, The Shubert Organization, Capital Cities/ABC, and The Royal National Theatre.
Stanley by Pam Gems. Produced by Circle in the Square, Gregory Mosher, and M. Edgar Rosenblum.
☆   *The Last Night of Ballyhoo* by Alfred Uhry. Produced by Jane Harmon, Nina Keneally, and Liz Oliver.
The Young Man from Atlanta by Horton Foote. Produced by David Richenthal, Anita Waxman, Jujamcyn Theaters, The

Goodman Theatre, and Robert Cole.

Revival (Play)

☆ A *Doll's House*. Produced by Bill Kenwright and Thelma Holt.

London Assurance. Produced by Roundabout Theatre Company,
Todd Haimes, and Ellen Richard.

Present Laughter. Produced by David Richenthal, Anita Waxman,
and Jujamcyn Theaters.

The Gin Game. Produced by National Actors Theatre and Tony
Randall.

Revival (Musical)

Annie. Produced by Timothy Childs, Rodger Hess, Jujamcyn
Theaters, Terri B. Childs, and Al Nocciolino.

Candide. Produced by Livent (U.S.) Inc.

☆ *Chicago*. Produced by Barry and Fran Weissler and Kardana
Productions Inc.

Once Upon a Mattress. Produced by Dodger Productions and Joop
van den Ende.

Leading Actor (Play)

Brian Bedford, *London Assurance*

Michael Gambon, *Skylight*

☆ Christopher Plummer, *Barrymore*

Antony Sher, *Stanley*

Leading Actress (Play)

Julie Harris, *The Gin Game*

Shirley Knight, *The Young Man from Atlanta*

☆ Janet McTeer, *A Doll's House*

Lia Williams, *Skylight*

Featured Actor (Play)

Terry Beaver, *The Last Night of Ballyhoo*

William Biff McGuire, *The Young Man from Atlanta*

Brian Murray, *The Little Foxes*

☆ Owen Teale, *A Doll's House*

Featured Actress (Play)

Helen Carey, *London Assurance*

Dana Ivey, *The Last Night of Ballyhoo*

☆ Lynne Thigpen, *An American Daughter*

Celia Weston, *The Last Night of Ballyhoo*

Leading Actor (Musical)

Robert Cuccioli, *Jekyll & Hyde*

Jim Dale, *Candide*

Daniel McDonald, *Steel Pier*
☆ James Naughton, *Chicago*

LEADING ACTRESS (MUSICAL)
Pamela Isaacs, *The Life*
☆ Bebe Neuwirth, *Chicago*
Tonya Pinkins, *Play On!*
Karen Ziemba, *Steel Pier*

FEATURED ACTOR (MUSICAL)
Joel Blum, *Steel Pier*
☆ Chuck Cooper, *The Life*
André De Shields, *Play On!*
Sam Harris, *The Life*

FEATURED ACTRESS (MUSICAL)
Marcia Lewis, *Chicago*
Andrea Martin, *Candide*
Debra Monk, *Steel Pier*
☆ Lillias White, *The Life*

DIRECTOR (PLAY)
John Caird, *Stanley*
Richard Eyre, *Skylight*
☆ Anthony Page, A *Doll's House*
Charles Nelson Reilly, *The Gin Game*

DIRECTOR (MUSICAL)
Michael Blakemore, *The Life*
☆ Walter Bobbie, *Chicago*
Scott Ellis, *Steel Pier*
Julie Taymor, *Juan Darién, A Carnival Mass*

BOOK (MUSICAL)
Jekyll & Hyde by Leslie Bricusse
Steel Pier by David Thompson
The Life by David Newman, Ira Gasman, Cy Coleman
☆ *Titanic* by Peter Stone

SCORE
Juan Darién, A Carnival Mass. Music and lyrics by Elliot Goldenthal.
Steel Pier. Music by John Kander, lyrics by Fred Ebb.
The Life. Music by Cy Coleman, lyrics by Ira Gasman.
☆ *Titanic*. Music and lyrics by Maury Yeston.

ORCHESTRATIONS
Michael Gibson, *Steel Pier*

Luther Henderson, *Play On!*
Don Sebesky and Harold Wheeler, *The Life*
☆ Jonathan Tunick, *Titanic*

SCENIC DESIGNER
John Lee Beatty, *The Little Foxes*
☆ Stewart Laing, *Titanic*
G.W. Mercier and Julie Taymor, *Juan Darién, A Carnival Mass*
Tony Walton, *Steel Pier*

COSTUME DESIGNER
Ann Curtis, *Jekyll & Hyde*
☆ Judith Dolan, *Candide*
William Ivey Long, *Chicago*
Martin Pakledinaz, *The Life*

LIGHTING DESIGNER
☆ Ken Billington, *Chicago*
Beverly Emmons, *Jekyll & Hyde*
Donald Holder, *Juan Darién, A Carnival Mass*
Richard Pilbrow, *The Life*

CHOREOGRAPHER
Wayne Cilento, *Dream*
Joey McKneely, *The Life*
☆ Ann Reinking, *Chicago*
Susan Stroman, *Steel Pier*

REGIONAL THEATRE
☆ Berkeley Repertory Theatre, Berkeley, California

1998

MUSICAL
Ragtime. Produced by LIVENT (U.S.) Inc.
Side Show. Produced by Emanuel Azenberg, Joseph Nederlander, Herschel Waxman, Janice McKenna, and Scott Nederlander.
☆ *The Lion King.* Produced by Disney.
The Scarlet Pimpernel. Produced by Pierre Cossette, Bill Haber, Hallmark Entertainment, Ted Forstmann, and Kathleen Raitt.

PLAY
☆ *Art* by Yasmina Reza. Produced by David Pugh, Sean Connery, and Joan Cullman.

Freak by John Leguizamo. Produced by Arielle Tepper, Bill Haber, and Gregory Mosher.

Golden Child by David Henry Hwang. Produced by Benjamin Mordecai, Dori Bernstein, John Kao, John F. Kennedy Center for the Performing Arts, South Coast Repertory, The Joseph Papp Public Theater/New York Shakespeare Festival, and American Conservatory Theater.

The Beauty Queen of Leenane by Martin McDonagh, Produced by Atlantic Theater Company, Randall L. Wreghitt, Chase Mishkin, Steven M. Levy, Leonard Soloway, Julian Schlossberg, Norma Langworthy, and The Druid Theatre Company/Royal Court Theatre.

REVIVAL (PLAY)

☆ A *View from the Bridge.* Produced by Roundabout Theatre Company, Todd Haimes, Ellen Richard, Roger Berlind, James M. Nederlander, Nathaniel Kramer, Elizabeth Ireland McCann, Roy Gabay, and Old Ivy Productions.

Ah, Wilderness! Producers: Lincoln Center Theater, André Bishop, and Bernard Gersten.

The Chairs. Produced by Bill Kenwright, Carole Shorenstein Hays, Scott Rudin, Stuart Thompson, and Théâtre de Complicité/Royal Court Theatre.

The Diary of Anne Frank. Produced by David Stone, Amy Nederlander- Case, Jon B. Platt, Jujamcyn Theaters, Hal Luftig, Harriet Newman Leve, and James D. Stern.

REVIVAL (MUSICAL)

☆ *Cabaret.* Produced by Roundabout Theatre Company, Todd Haimes, and Ellen Richard.

1776. Produced by Roundabout Theatre Company, Todd Haimes, Ellen Richard, James M. Nederlander, Stewart F. Lane, Rodger Hess, Bill Haber, Robert Halmi Jr., Dodger Endemol Theatricals, and Hallmark Entertainment.

The Sound of Music. Produced by Thomas Viertel, Steven Baruch, Richard Frankel, Jujamcyn Theaters, The Rodgers and Hammerstein Organization, Charles Kelman Productions, Simone Genatt Haft, Marc Routh, Jay Binder, and Robert Halmi, Jr.

LEADING ACTOR (PLAY)

Richard Briers, *The Chairs*
☆ Anthony LaPaglia, A *View from the Bridge*
John Leguizamo, *Freak*
Alfred Molina, *Art*

LEADING ACTRESS (PLAY)

Jane Alexander, *Honour*
Allison Janney, A *View from the Bridge*
Geraldine McEwan, *The Chairs*
☆ Marie Mullen, *The Beauty Queen of Leenane*

FEATURED ACTOR (PLAY)

☆ Tom Murphy, *The Beauty Queen of Leenane*
Brian F. O'Byrne, *The Beauty Queen of Leenane*
Sam Trammell, A*h, Wilderness!*
Max Wright, *Ivanov*

FEATURED ACTRESS (PLAY)

Enid Graham, *Honour*
Linda Lavin, *The Diary of Anne Frank*
☆ Anna Manahan, *The Beauty Queen of Leenane*
Julyana Soelistyo, *Golden Child*

LEADING ACTOR (MUSICAL)

☆ Alan Cumming, *Cabaret*
Peter Friedman, *Ragtime*
Brian Stokes Mitchell, *Ragtime*
Douglas Sills, *The Scarlet Pimpernel*

LEADING ACTRESS (MUSICAL)

Betty Buckley, *Triumph of Love*
Marin Mazzie, *Ragtime*
☆ Natasha Richardson, *Cabaret*
Alice Ripley and Emily Skinner, *Side Show*

FEATURED ACTOR (MUSICAL)

Gregg Edelman, *1776*
John McMartin, *High Society*
☆ Ron Rifkin, *Cabaret*
Samuel E. Wright, *The Lion King*

FEATURED ACTRESS (MUSICAL)

Anna Kendrick, *High Society*
Tsidii Le Loka, *The Lion King*
☆ Audra McDonald, *Ragtime*
Mary Louise Wilson, *Cabaret*

DIRECTOR (PLAY)

☆ Garry Hynes, *The Beauty Queen of Leenane*
Michael Mayer, A *View from the Bridge*
Simon McBurney, *The Chairs*
Matthew Warchus, *Art*

DIRECTOR (MUSICAL)
Scott Ellis, 1776
Frank Galati, *Ragtime*
Sam Mendes with Rob Marshall, *Cabaret*
☆ Julie Taymor, *The Lion King*

BOOK (MUSICAL)
☆ *Ragtime* by Terrence McNally
Side Show by Bill Russell
The Lion King by Roger Allers and Irene Mecchi
The Scarlet Pimpernel by Nan Knighton

SCORE
☆ *Ragtime*. Music by Stephen Flaherty, lyrics by Lynn Ahrens.
Side Show. Music by Henry Krieger, lyrics by Bill Russell.
The Capeman. Music by Paul Simon, lyrics by Derek Walcott.
The Lion King, Music and lyrics by Elton John, Tim Rice, Lebo M.,
      Mark Mancina, Jay Rifkin, Julie Taymor, and Hans Zimmer.

ORCHESTRATIONS
☆ William David Brohn, *Ragtime*
Robert Elhai, David Metzger, Bruce Fowler, *The Lion King*
Michael Gibson, *Cabaret*
Stanley Silverman, *The Capeman*

SCENIC DESIGNER
Bob Crowley, *The Capeman*
☆ Richard Hudson, *The Lion King*
Eugene Lee, *Ragtime*
Quay Brothers, *The Chairs*

COSTUME DESIGNER
William Ivey Long, *Cabaret*
Santo Loquasto, *Ragtime*
Martin Pakledinaz, *Golden Child*
☆ Julie Taymor, *The Lion King*

LIGHTING DESIGNER
Paul Anderson, *The Chairs*
Peggy Eisenhauer, Mike Baldassari, *Cabaret*
Jules Fisher, Peggy Eisenhauer, *Ragtime*
☆ Donald Holder, *The Lion King*

CHOREOGRAPHER
Graciela Daniele, *Ragtime*
☆ Garth Fagan, *The Lion King*
Forever Tango Dancers, *Luis Bravo's Forever Tango*

Rob Marshall, *Cabaret*

REGIONAL THEATRE
☆ Denver Center Theatre Company, Denver, Colorado

SPECIAL AWARDS
☆ Lifetime Achievement: Edward E. Colton
☆ Lifetime Achievement: Ben Edwards

TONY HONOR
☆ International Theatre Institute of the United States and Martha Coigney, Director

1999

MUSICAL
The Civil War. Producered by Pierre Cossette, PACE Theatrical Group / SFX Entertainment, Bomurwil Productions, Kathleen Raitt, and Jujamcyn Theaters.
☆ Fosse. Produced by Livent (U.S.) Inc.
It Ain't Nothin' But the Blues. Produced by Eric Krebs, Jonathan Reinis, Lawrence Horowitz, Anita Waxman, Elizabeth Williams, CTM Productions, Anne Squadron, Lincoln Center Theatre, Crossroads Theatre Company, San Diego Repertory Theatre, and Alabama Shakespeare Festival.
Parade. Produced by Lincoln Center Theatre, André Bishop, Bernard Gersten, and Livent (U.S.) Inc.

PLAY
Closer by Patrick Marber. Produced by Robert Fox, Scott Rudin, Roger Berlind, Carole Shorenstein Hays, ABC Inc., The Shubert Organization, and The Royal National Theatre.
The Lonesome West by Martin McDonagh. Produced by Randall L. Wreghitt, Steven M. Levy, Norma Langworthy, Gayle Francis, Dani Davis and Jason Howland, Loan Stein and Susan Dietz, Everett King, PACE Theatrical Group/SFX Entertainment/Jon B. Platt, and The Druid Theatre Company/Royal Court Theatre.
Not About Nightingales by Tennessee Williams. Produced by Carole Shorenstein Hays, Stuart Thompson, Marsha Garces Williams, Kelly Gonda, Royal National Theatre, Alley Theatre, and Moving Theatre.
☆ Side Man by Warren Leight. Produced by Jay Harris/Weissberger Theatre Group, Peter Manning, Roundabout Theatre Company, Todd Haimes, Ellen Richard, Ron Kastner, James Cushing, and Joan Stein.

REVIVAL (PLAY)

☆ *Death of a Salesman* by Arthur Miller. Produced by David Richenthal, Jujamcyn Theaters, Allan S. Gordon, Fox Theatricals, Jerry Frankel, and The Goodman Theatre.

Electra by Sophocles, adapted by Frank McGuinness. Produced by Eric Krebs, Randall L. Wreghitt, Anita Waxman, Elizabeth Williams, Lawrence Horowitz, McCarter Theatre/Donmar Warehouse, and Duncan C. Weldon.

The Iceman Cometh by Eugene O'Neill. Produced by Allan S. Gordon, Bill Haber, Ira Pittelman, Elan McAllister, Trigger Street Productions, and Emanuel Azenberg.

Twelfth Night by William Shakespeare. Produced by Lincoln Center Theatre, André Bishop, and Bernard Gersten.

REVIVAL (MUSICAL)

☆ *Annie Get Your Gun.* Produced by Barry and Fran Weissler, Kardana, Michael Watt, Irving Welzer, and Hal Luftig.

Little Me. Produced by Roundabout Theatre Company, Todd Haimes, Ellen Richard, and Julia C. Levy.

Peter Pan. Produced by McCoy Rigby Entertainment, The Nederlander Organization, La Mirada Theatre for the Performing Arts, Albert Nocciolino, Larry Payton, and J. Lynn Singleton.

You're a Good Man, Charlie Brown. Produced by Michael Leavitt, Fox Theatricals, Jerry Frankel, Arthur Whitelaw, and Gene Persson.

LEADING ACTOR (PLAY)

☆ Brian Dennehy, *Death of a Salesman*
Brían O'Byrne, *The Lonesome West*
Corin Redgrave, *Not About Nightingales*
Kevin Spacey, *The Iceman Cometh*

LEADING ACTRESS (PLAY)

Stockard Channing, *The Lion in Winter*
☆ Judi Dench, *Amy's View*
Marian Seldes, *Ring Round the Moon*
Zoë Wanamaker, *Electra*

FEATURED ACTOR (PLAY)

Kevin Anderson, *Death of a Salesman*
Finbar Lynch, *Not About Nightingales*
Howard Witt, *Death of a Salesman*
☆ Frank Wood, *Sideman*

FEATURED ACTRESS (PLAY)
Claire Bloom, *Electra*
Samantha Bond, *Amy's View*
Dawn Bradfield, *The Lonesome West*
☆   Elizabeth Franz, *Death of a Salesman*

LEADING ACTOR (MUSICAL)
Brent Carver, *Parade*
Adam Cooper, *Swan Lake*
☆   Martin Short, *Little Me*
Tom Wopat, *Annie Get Your Gun*

LEADING ACTRESS (MUSICAL)
Carolee Carmello, *Parade*
Dee Hoty, *Footloose*
☆   Bernadette Peters, *Annie Get Your Gun*
Sîan Phillips, *Marlene*

FEATURED ACTOR (MUSICAL)
☆   Roger Bart, *You're a Good Man, Charlie Brown*
Desmond Richardson, *Fosse*
Ron Taylor, *It Ain't Nothin' But the Blues*
Scott Wise, *Fosse*

FEATURED ACTRESS (MUSICAL)
Greta Boston, *It Ain't Nothin But the Blues*
☆   Kristin Chenoweth, *You're a Good Man, Charlie Brown*
Valarie Pettiford, *Fosse*
Mary Testa, *On the Town*

DIRECTION (PLAY)
Howard Davies, *The Iceman Cometh*
☆   Robert Falls, *Death of a Salesman*
Garry Hynes, *The Lonesome West*
Trevor Nunn, *Not About Nightingales*

DIRECTION (MUSICAL)
☆   Matthew Bourne, *Swan Lake*
Richard Maltby, Jr. and Ann Reinking, *Fosse*
Michael Mayer, *You're a Good Man, Charlie Brown*
Harold Prince, *Parade*

BOOK (MUSICAL)
Footloose by Dean Pitchford and Walter Bobbie
It Ain't Nothin' But the Blues by Charles Bevel, Lita Gaithers,
      Randal Myler, Ron Taylor, and Dan Wheetman
Marlene by Pam Gems

☆　*Parade* by Alfred Uhry

SCORE

Footloose. Music and lyrics by Tom Snow, Dean Pitchford, Erin Carmen, Sammy Hagar, Kenny Loggins, and Jim Steinman.
☆　*Parade*. Music and lyrics by Jason Robert Brown.
The Civil War. Music by Frank Wildhorn, lyrics by Jack Murphy.
Twelfth Night. Music by Jeanine Tesori.

ORCHESTRATIONS

☆　Ralph Burns and Douglas Besterman, *Fosse*
David Cullen, *Swan Lake*
Don Sebesky, *Parade*
Harold Wheeler, *Little Me*

SCENIC DESIGN

Bob Crowley, *The Iceman Cometh*
Bob Crowley, *Twelfth Night*
Riccardo Hernandez, *Parade*
☆　Richard Hoover, *Not About Nightingales*

COSTUME DESIGN

☆　Lez Brotherston, *Swan Lake*
Santo Loquasto, *Fosse*
John David Ridge, *Ring Round the Moon*
Catherine Zuber, *Twelfth Night*

LIGHTING DESIGN

☆　Andrew Bridge, *Fosse*
Mark Henderson, *The Iceman Cometh*
Natasha Katz, *Twelfth Night*
Chris Parry, *Not About Nightingales*

CHOREOGRAPHY

Patricia Birch, *Parade*
☆　Matthew Bourne, *Swan Lake*
A.C. Ciulla, *Footloose*
Rob Marshall, *Little Me*

REGIONAL THEATRE

☆　Crossroads Theatre Company, New Brunswick, New Jersey

SPECIAL AWARD

☆　Lifetime Achievement: Uta Hagen
☆　Lifetime Achievement: Isabelle Stevenson
☆　Lifetime Achievement: Arthur Miller
☆　*Fool Moon*

The 2000s

"Now that I have won a Tony Award, the question I seem to be getting the most lately is, "Where are you going to put it?" I have often seen them placed on high shelves where they are rarely moved or touched, but I don't think that's for me.

I look forward to letting it hit the road and tour with people that have helped me get where I am—my family, my friends, my teachers. I also want to share it with the students that I often speak to who desire a life in the theatre. I would like them to see it and touch it and clutch it to themselves and to feel that it is also within their grasp.

For me, the REAL Tony Award is more esoteric. It is a title that forever after lives with your name—"Tony winner so-and-so." It is a concept that doesn't change you so much as it changes the way people perceive you. It is a symbol of all of the shows you have done and the people you have worked with and learned from. My Tony will be found in my mind and in my heart.

—Brian Stokes Mitchell
Actor (Musical), *Kiss Me, Kate*

2000

MUSICAL

☆ *Contact.* Produced by Lincoln Center Theatre, André Bishop, and Bernard Gersten.

James Joyce's The Dead. Produced by Gregory Mosher, Arielle Tepper, Playwrights Horizons, and Tim Sanford.

Swing! Produced by Marc Routh, Richard Frankel, Steven Baruch, Tom Viertel, Lorie Cowen Levy/Stanley Shopkorn, Jujamcyn Theaters, BB Promotion, Dede Harris/Jeslo Productions, Libby Adler Mages/Mari Glick, Douglas L. Meyer/James D. Stern, and PACE Theatrical Group/SFX.

The Wild Party. Produced by The Joseph Papp Public Theatre/New York Shakespeare Festival, George C. Wolfe, Scott Rudin/Paramount Pictures, Roger Berlind, and Williams/Waxman.

PLAY

☆ *Copenhagen* by Michael Frayn. Produced by Michael Codron, Lee Dean, The Royal National Theatre, James M. Nederlander, Roger Berlind, Scott Rudin, Elizabeth Ireland McCann, Ray Larsen, Jon B. Platt, Byron Goldman, and Scott Nederlander.

Dirty Blonde by Claudia Shear. Produced by The Shubert Organization, Chase Mishkin, Ostar Enterprises ABC, Inc., and New York Theatre Workshop.

The Ride Down Mt. Morgan by Arthur Miller. Produced by The Shubert Organization, Scott Rudin, Roger Berlind, Spring Sirkin, ABC Inc., The Public Theatre/New York Shakespeare Festival, and George C. Wolfe.

True West by Sam Shepard. Produced by Ron Kastner.

REVIVAL (PLAY)

A Moon for the Misbegotten by Eugene O'Neill. Produced by Elliot Martin, Chase Mishkin, Max Cooper, and Jujamcyn Theaters in association with Anita Waxman, Elizabeth Williams, and The Goodman Theatre.

Amadeus by Peter Shaffer. Produced by Kim Poster, PW Productions, Adam Epstein, SFX Theatrical Group, and Center Theatre Group/Ahmanson Theatre in association with Back Row Productions, and Old Ivy Productions.

The Price by Arthur Miller. Produced by David Richenthal.

☆ *The Real Thing* by Tom Stoppard. Produced by Anita Waxman,

Elizabeth Williams, Ron Kastner, and Miramax Films present The Donmar Warehouse Production.

REVIVAL (MUSICAL)

Jesus Christ Superstar. Produced by The Really Useful Superstar Company Inc., The Nederlander Producing Company of America Inc., and Terry Allen Kramer.

☆　*Kiss Me, Kate*. Produced by Roger Berlind and Roger Horchow.

Meredith Willson's The Music Man. Produced by Dodger Theatricals, The John F. Kennedy Center for the Performing Arts, Elizabeth Williams/Anita Waxman, Kardana-Swinsky, and Lorie Cowen Levy/Dede Harris.

Tango Argentino. Produced by DG Producciones.

LEADING ACTOR (PLAY)

Gabriel Byrne, A *Moon for the Misbegotten*
☆　Stephen Dillane, *The Real Thing*
Philip Seymour Hoffman, *True West*
John C. Reilly, *True West*
David Suchet, *Amadeus*

LEADING ACTRESS (PLAY)

Jayne Atkinson, *The Rainmaker*
☆　Jennifer Ehle, *The Real Thing*
Rosemary Harris, *Waiting in the Wings*
Cherry Jones, A *Moon for the Misbegotten*
Claudia Shear, *Dirty Blonde*

FEATURED ACTOR (PLAY)

Kevin Chamberlin, *Dirty Blonde*
Daniel Davis, *Wrong Mountain*
☆　Roy Dotrice, A *Moon for the Misbegotten*
Derek Smith, *The Green Bird*
Bob Stillman, *Dirty Blonde*

FEATURED ACTRESS (PLAY)

☆　Blair Brown, *Copenhagen*
Frances Conroy, *The Ride Down Mt. Morgan*
Amy Ryan, *Uncle Vanya*
Helen Stenborg, *Waiting in the Wings*
Sarah Woodward, *The Real Thing*

LEADING ACTOR (MUSICAL)

Craig Bierko, *Meredith Willson's The Music Man*
George Hearn, *Putting It Together*

☆ Brian Stokes Mitchell, Kiss Me, Kate
Mandy Patinkin, The Wild Party
Christopher Walken, James Joyce's The Dead

LEADING ACTRESS (MUSICAL)
Toni Collette, The Wild Party
☆ Heather Headley, AIDA
Rebecca Luker, Meredith Willson's The Music Man
Marin Mazzie, Kiss Me, Kate
Audra McDonald, Marie Christine

FEATURED ACTOR (MUSICAL)
Michael Berresse, Kiss Me, Kate
☆ Boyd Gaines, Contact
Michael Mulheren, Kiss Me, Kate
Stephen Spinella, James Joyce's The Dead
Lee Wilkof, Kiss Me, Kate

FEATURED ACTRESS (MUSICAL)
Laura Benanti, Swing!
Ann Hampton Callaway, Swing!
Eartha Kitt, The Wild Party
Deborah Yates, Contact
☆ Karen Ziemba, Contact

DIRECTION (PLAY)
☆ Michael Blakemore, Copenhagen
James Lapine, Dirty Blonde
David Leveaux, The Real Thing
Matthew Warchus, True West

DIRECTION (MUSICAL)
☆ Michael Blakemore, Kiss Me, Kate
Susan Stroman, Contact
Susan Stroman, Meredith Willson's The Music Man
Lynne Taylor-Corbett, Swing!

BOOK (MUSICAL)
Contact by John Weidman.
☆ James Joyce's The Dead by Richard Nelson.
Marie Christine by Michael John LaChiusa.
The Wild Party by Michael John LaChiusa and George C. Wolfe.

SCORE
☆ AIDA. Music by Elton John, lyrics by Tim Rice.
James Joyce's The Dead. Music by Shaun Davey, lyrics by Richard
    Nelson and Shaun Davey.

Marie Christine. Music and lyrics by Michael John LaChiusa.
The Wild Party. Music and lyrics by Michael John LaChiusa.

ORCHESTRATIONS

Doug Besterman, *Meredith Willson's The Music Man*
☆ Don Sebesky, *Kiss Me, Kate*
Jonathan Tunick, *Marie Christine*
Harold Wheeler, *Swing!*

SCENIC DESIGN

☆ Bob Crowley, *AIDA*
Thomas Lynch, *Meredith Willson's The Music Man*
Robin Wagner, *Kiss Me, Kate*
Tony Walton, *Uncle Vanya*

COSTUME DESIGN

Bob Crowley, *AIDA*
Constance Hoffman, *The Green Bird*
William Ivey Long, *Meredith Willson's The Music Man*
☆ Martin Pakledinaz, *Kiss Me, Kate*

LIGHTING DESIGN

Jules Fisher and Peggy Eisenhauer, *The Wild Party*
Jules Fisher and Peggy Eisenhauer, *Marie Christine*
Peter Kaczorowski, *Kiss Me, Kate*
☆ Natasha Katz, *AIDA*

CHOREOGRAPHY

Kathleen Marshall, *Kiss Me, Kate*
☆ Susan Stroman, *Contact*
Susan Stroman, *Meredith Willson's The Music Man*
Lynne Taylor-Corbett, *Swing!*

REGIONAL THEATRE

☆ Utah Shakespearean Festival of Cedar City, Utah

SPECIAL AWARDS

☆ Lifetime Achievement: T. Edward Hambleton
☆ Special Theatrical Event: *Dame Edna: The Royal Tour*

TONY HONORS

☆ Eileen Heckart
☆ Sylvia Herscher
☆ *City Center Encores!*

Rules and Regulations of the American Theatre Wing's Tony Awards 2000–01 Season

The following are the Tony Awards Rules and Regulations for the 2000-2001 theatrical season (the "*Rules*"). These Rules are intended to apply to that season, do not necessarily reflect prior practice or custom, and are subject to change without notice.

1. ADMINISTRATION

    (a) The Antoinette Perry (Tony) Awards Administration Committee (the "*Tony Awards Administration Committee*") shall administer the American Theatre Wing's Tony Awards, pursuant to the rules of governance established from time to time by the Tony Awards Management Committee appointed by American Theatre Wing, Inc. (the "*Wing*") and The League of American Theatres and Producers, Inc. (the "*League*"). The provisions of paragraphs 1(b) through 1(d) below set forth the current rules of governance.

    (b) The Tony Awards Administration Committee shall be a

self-governing body comprised of 24 members, of whom 10 shall be designees of the Wing, 10 shall be designees of the League and one member shall be designated by each of The Dramatists Guild, Inc., Actors' Equity Association, United Scenic Artists, and Society of Stage Directors and Choreographers. The Wing and the League may also each designate an additional member on an *ex officio* basis, such additional members to be entitled to attend meetings of the Tony Awards Administration Committee and to participate in all discussions and deliberations thereat, but not to vote. Proxies are not permitted in any vote of the Tony Awards Administration Committee; however, in order to provide continuity, the Wing and the League shall each appoint up to five alternate designees and each of the other organizations represented on the Tony Awards Administration Committee shall each appoint one alternate designee. Each of the alternate designees shall have the right to attend Tony Awards Administration Committee meetings, but shall not have the right to speak or vote at such meetings unless such alternate designee's principal designee shall be unable to attend (it being understood, in the case of the Wing and the League, that their alternates shall serve in a pre-designated order, in the event of the absence of any of their respective principal designees), in which case the vote of such alternate shall be valid and binding as if made by the alternate's principal designee. All persons to be designated to serve as members, alternates or additional members *ex officio* of the Tony Awards Administration Committee shall be so designated (in a writing delivered by the designating organization to the Tony Awards Management Committee) no later than the June 15th immediately preceding the season for which such persons are designated.

(c) The Tony Awards Administration Committee shall meet from time to time and, among other duties, shall have the responsibility of determining eligibility for nominations in all award categories. In order to take any action there must be a quorum consisting of at least 16 members of the Tony Awards Administration Committee. In order to be eligible for nomination, a potential candidate for nomination must receive an affirmative vote of a majority of those members present. Any other action (including giving a Special Tony Award or Tony Honor for Excellence in the Theatre, but exclusive of changes in or waivers of these Rules or appointment to the Nominating Committee as provided below) shall require the affirmative vote of two-thirds of those members present. Changes in or waivers of these Rules shall require at least 16 votes; *provided, however*, that only the Tony Awards Management Committee may make changes in or waivers of the provisions of this paragraph 1; and *provided, further,* that no Rule may be waived other than for "good cause" shown. Appointment to the Nominating Committee shall require the affirmative vote of a majority of those members present.

(d) Any person outside the Tony Awards Administration Committee may request the Committee to take specific action in respect to any matter before the Committee, but the Committee may only consider such request if made in writing and in advance of the taking of action by the Committee. No such person shall be permitted to appear before the Committee.

(e)All decisions of the Tony Awards Administration Committee concerning eligibility for the Awards and all other matters relating to their administration, including adoption of amendments to these Rules (except as reserved to the Tony Award Management Committee above), shall be final, binding and conclusive for all purposes. All decisions of the Tony Awards Administration Committee and the Tony Awards Management Committee, as the case may be, regarding the interpretation of any Rule within their respective purview as provided herein shall be final, binding and conclusive for all purposes. No specific vote properly taken in accordance with these Rules may be retaken, at the same or any other meeting.

2. ELIGIBILITY FOR NOMINATION

(a)In order for the Tony Awards Administration Committee to determine that a production is eligible in the various categories for nomination for a Tony Award, all of the following six requirements must be satisfied:

i)   the production must be, in the judgment of the Tony Awards Administration Committee, a legitimate theatrical production

ii)   which *"officially opens"* (as defined in paragraph 2(e) herein)

iii) in an *"eligible Broadway theatre"* (as set forth on Exhibit A)

iv)   on or before the *"Eligibility Date"* of the current season (as defined in paragraph 2(e) herein), and after the Eligibility Date for the prior season

v)   the producer of the production must invite, in a timely manner and free of charge, each of the eligible Tony voters to attend a performance of the production. Invitations shall be extended, in a manner prescribed by the Tony Awards Administration Committee, for performances occurring no later than 16 weeks after the production officially opens or before the Thursday prior to the presentation of the Awards, whichever occurs first. For this purpose, the producer must make available at least eight "paid performances" of the production (i.e. previews, opening and/or regular performances in an eligible Broadway theatre). This requirement shall be subject to the following exception: If a production which officially opens in an eligible Broadway theatre on or before the Eligibility Date is unable to satisfy the eight paid performance requirement because it closes prior to presenting eight paid performances, the production may nevertheless be deemed eligible *provided that* the producer has invited and made tickets available to the Tony voters for at least one-half of all paid performances presented in an eligible Broadway theatre prior to the closing; and

vi) the producer must certify to (and on a form provided by) the Tony Awards Administration Committee (which must receive such certification prior to the Eligibility Date or within 16 weeks after the production officially opens, whichever occurs first) that the producer: (A) has fully complied with the Rules of the Tony Awards Administration Committee regarding the invitation of Tony voters; (B) accepts the authority of the Tony Awards Administration Committee to make all decisions or determinations concerning eligibility for the Awards and all other matters relating to their administration (including adopting amendments to these Rules) in its sole and absolute discretion (and without obligation to make any decision or determination consistent with any prior practice or custom), with the effect of any such decision or determination as final, binding and conclusive for all purposes; (C) accepts the authority of the Tony Awards Management Committee to make all decisions or determinations concerning the telecast of the Awards and all other matters relating to their administration not delegated to the Tony Awards Administration Committee (including adopting amendments to these Rules) in its sole and absolute discretion (and without obligation to make any decision or determination consistent with any prior practice or custom), with the effect of any such decision or determination as final, binding and conclusive for all purposes; (D) accepts the authority of the Nominating Committee to make all decisions or determinations concerning nominations for the Awards as provided herein (and without obligation to make any decision or determination consistent with any prior practice or custom), with the effect of any such decision or determination as final, binding and conclusive for all purposes; (E) accepts the authority of the Tony Awards voters to vote for the winners of the Awards with the effect of any such vote as final, binding and conclusive for all purposes; (F) will fully comply with the rules of the Tony Awards Management Committee (promulgated by Tony Award Productions) regarding the use of the Tony Awards trademarks and other intellectual property and material, as in effect from time to time; (G) shall not institute any action, suit or proceeding against the Tony Awards Administration Committee, the Tony Awards Management Committee, the Nominating Committee, any member of the foregoing committees, any entity or organization appointing any of person to any of such committees or any Tony Awards voter (in such capacity) for any purpose in connection with the Awards; and (H) shall indemnify, defend and hold harmless such committees, such members, such entities and organizations from and against any and all costs, expenses, damages, liabilities, claims and demands of any kind or nature (including without limitation attorneys' fees and disbursements and court costs) arising out of any such action, suit or proceeding commenced by such producer or by any other producer or producing firm or entity with respect to such production or any element thereof.

(b) *Eligibility as Best Play/Musical.* Any production of a play or musical (other than a "classic" as defined in paragraph 2(h) hereof) that has been presented professionally during or after the 1946-47 Broadway season in the Borough of Manhattan, but *not* in an eligible Broadway theatre, which current production meets the requirements of paragraph 2(a) hereof, shall be eligible to receive a nomination in the category of Best Play or Best Musical, as the case may be.

(c) *Substantial Duplication.* In order for a production to be eligible in the category of Best Play or Best Musical, a play or musical may contain elements that substantially duplicate elements of productions previously presented in an eligible Broadway theatre only if, in the judgment of the Tony Awards Administration Committee in each case, the duplicated and the original elements, in their totality, create a new play or musical.

(d) *Ineligibility of Production/Eligibility of Elements.* If a production meets the requirements of paragraphs 2(a) or 2(b) hereof, but is determined not to be eligible in the category of Best Play or Best Musical in accordance with paragraph 2(c) hereof (i.e., that such paragraph does apply, and a determination has been made by the Tony Awards Administration Committee thereunder that a new play or musical has not been created for purposes hereof), the production shall automatically be ineligible to receive a nomination in the category of Best Play or Best Musical; provided, however, that the ineligibility of the production to receive a nomination in the category of Best Play or Best Musical shall not adversely affect the eligibility of any of the individual elements (i.e., actors, actresses, playwrights, bookwriters, composers, lyricists, designers, directors, choreographers and orchestrators) who are otherwise eligible to receive nominations or awards in their respective categories.

(e)*Definitions.* For the purposes of these Rules, the term *"official opening"* shall mean the performance of the production which the producer has publicly announced as being the official opening; the term *"Eligibility Date"* shall mean the date which the Tony Awards Management Committee establishes as the cut-off date for eligibility; and the term *"Submission Date"* shall mean the date that is 14 days prior to the Eligibility Date. The Eligibility Date for the current season shall be at least 32 days prior to the date on which the Awards are to be presented.

(f) *Theatres.* In order to qualify as an eligible Broadway theatre, a theatre must (i) have 500 or more seats, (ii) be used principally for the presentation of legitimate theatrical productions and (iii) be deemed otherwise qualified by the Tony Awards Administration Committee. A list of eligible Broadway theatres for the current season is attached hereto as Exhibit A. A theatre may be added to such list with respect to a particular season only by action of the Tony Awards Administration Committee, which shall consider all requests to add theatres made by the Submission Date of the immediately preceding season, and issue any changes to Exhibit A by the June 15th immediately following such date.

(g)*Classics.* A play or musical that is determined by the Tony Awards Administration Committee (in its sole discretion) to be a *"classic"* shall not be eligible for an Award in the Best Play or Best Musical category but may be eligible in the appropriate Best Revival category, if any, provided it meets all other eligibility requirements set forth in these Rules.

(h) *Revivals.* Each year the Tony Awards Administration Committee shall determine whether there shall exist in quality and quantity a sufficient number of Revivals to merit the granting of an Award for Best Revival of a Play or Musical and, if so, the Tony Awards Administration Committee shall also determine whether there shall be a separate Play and Musical Revival category; *provided, however*, that if there are at least three such plays and three such musicals, there shall automatically be separate Play and Musical Revival categories. A *"Revival"* shall be any production in an eligible

Broadway theatre of a play or musical that: (A) is deemed a "classic" in accordance with paragraph 2(g) above; (B) was previously presented professionally at any time prior to the 1946-47 Broadway season in substantially the same form in the Borough of Manhattan (other than as a showcase, workshop or so-called "letter of agreement" production) and that has not had a professional performance in the Borough of Manhattan at any time during the three years immediately preceding the Eligibility Date; or (C) was previously presented professionally at any time during or after the 1946–47 Broadway season in substantially the same form in an eligible Broadway theatre and that has not had a professional performance in the Borough of Manhattan at any time during the three years immediately preceding the Eligibility Date. The determination that a play or musical is ineligible in the category of Best Play or Best Musical shall not, in and of itself, make the play or musical eligible in a Best Revival category unless the play or musical also meets the requirements of this paragraph. Regardless of whether a production of a play or musical is eligible for a Best Revival category, the elements of the production shall be eligible in those categories in which said elements do not, in the judgment of the Tony Awards Administration Committee, substantially duplicate any prior presentation of the play or musical; provided, that the play or musical otherwise meets all the requirements set forth herein for Revivals.

(i) *Producers.* The producers eligible for nomination for a Tony Award shall include those producers listed above the title in the opening night program for a production together with any other producers as may be approved by the Tony Awards Administration Committee consistent with its usual policies.

(j) *Determination of Eligible Candidates for Nomination.* (A) The Tony Awards Administration Committee shall submit to the Nominating Committee (as described in paragraph 5 herein) a list of the eligible candidates for nomination in each Award category. The Tony Awards Administration Committee shall determine whether a sufficient number of eligible candidates exist in quality or quantity to merit the granting of an Award in the applicable category for the current season. If there is only one such eligible candidate for any category, the Tony Awards Administration Committee shall submit such candidate to the Nominating Committee pursuant to Paragraph 4(b) below. There shall be no more than four nominees in each category, other than the Best Performance categories, in which there shall be five nominees; *provided, however*, that the Tony Awards Administration Committee shall also have the sole discretion to reduce the number of nominees to fewer than four (or five), but, in no event, fewer than two in a particular category for the current season or to delegate this discretion to the Nominating Committee. Eligibility for nomination in the Best Performance categories shall be limited to one Actor or Actress for each nomination in such categories.

(B) In determining in which Award category any eligible candidate (person or production) shall be placed, the Tony Awards Administration Committee shall use the opening night program as its initial guide, together with any additional guidelines adopted by said Committee.

(1) If a producer of a particular production wishes to propose that an eligible candidate be placed in a category other than that indicated by the opening night program, the producer (whether or not a member of the Tony Awards Administration Committee) may send a written request to the Tony Awards Administration Committee setting forth the producer's reasons for asking the Committee to consider such a change. Such request cannot be considered if sent later than two weeks following the official opening of such production or the Eligibility Date, whichever occurs first.

(2) If any member of the Tony Awards Administration Committee who has an interest of any nature in a particular production, such member shall disclose such interest as early as possible, and, while maintaining such interest may not vote on such a proposed change (regardless of whether a request for such change has been timely made by the producer or by anyone else); *provided, however,* that such interested member may participate in discussions regarding such proposed change. The vote required to pass such a category change shall be a majority of those members present who are not ineligible to vote by reason of this paragraph. A member of the Committee shall not be ineligible to vote on a category change in a particular production if such member's sole interest of any nature in such production is that member's affiliation with the same union, guild or organization which has as one of its members, a person who has an interest of any nature in such production.

(3) Once the placement of an eligible candidate in a category has been decided by the Tony Awards Administration Committee, the placement cannot be changed at a later date.

(k) *Special Theatrical Events.* Each year the Tony Awards Administration Committee shall determine whether there shall exist in quality and quantity a sufficient number of Special

Theatrical Events to merit the granting of an Award for Special Theatrical Event. A "Special Theatrical Event" shall be any production in an eligible Broadway theatre that is, in the judgment of the Tony Awards Administration Committee, a live theatrical production that is not a play or musical.

3.   THE AWARDS PRESENTATION AND ELIGIBILITY DATE
     (a)The Awards shall be presented during the theatrical season but not earlier than May 24th of such season, unless otherwise determined by the Tony Awards Management Committee upon at least four months' notice prior to the date selected for such presentation. The date of the presentation ceremony shall be announced as soon as it has been determined.
     (b) The Eligibility Date for nominations shall be announced as soon as it has been determined.

4.   CATEGORIES OF AWARDS
     (a) The Awards may, subject to the provisions of these Rules, be made in the following categories:

     Best Play—Award to Author(s); Award to Producer(s)
     Best Musical—Award to Producer(s)
     Best Book of a Musical
     Best Original Score (Music & Lyrics) Written for the Theatre
     Best Performance by a leading Actor in a Play
     Best Performance by a leading Actress in a Play
     Best Performance by a leading Actor in a Musical
     Best Performance by a leading Actress in a Musical
     Best Performance by a featured Actor in a Play
     Best Performance by a featured Actress in a Play
     Best Performance by a featured Actor in a Musical
     Best Performance by a featured Actress in a Musical
     Best Direction of a Play
     Best Direction of a Musical
     Best Scenic Design
     Best Costume Design
     Best Lighting Design
     Best Choreography
     Best Revival of a Play or Musical (see Paragraph 2(h))
     Best Orchestration
     Special Theatrical Event (see Paragraph 2(k))

     (b) If the Tony Awards Administration Committee has determined that there is only one eligible candidate in a category listed in Paragraph 4(a) above, the Tony Awards Administration Committee shall submit such candidate to the Nominating Committee which may, by the vote of a majority of its members (according to a secret ballot), grant an Award in that category.

(c) The Tony Awards Administration Committee may, in its discretion, give a "Tony Award" to a regional theatre company upon the recommendation of the American Theatre Critics Association or another organization chosen by the Tony Awards Administration Committee, which organization shall apply objective and fair standards to determine that such regional theatre company has displayed a continuous level of artistic achievement contributing to the growth of theatre nationally.

(d) The Tony Awards Administration Committee may, in its discretion, give a "Special Tony Award" for lifetime achievement in the theatre.

(e) The Tony Awards Administration Committee may, in its discretion, give a "Special Tony Award" to a live theatrical event that "officially opens" in an "eligible Broadway theatre" on or before the "Eligibility Date" of the current season, but which does not fit into any other category of Tony Award to be awarded for the current season, which "Special Tony Award" shall be designated to be awarded to the production or any element thereof, unless such element is otherwise determined to be eligible in another existing Tony Award category in accordance with paragraph 2(d) hereof.

(f) Each Tony Award winner in the categories listed in Paragraph 4(a) above and each recipient of the Regional Theatre Tony Award and Special Tony Awards, and no other persons, will be entitled to receive from the Tony Awards Administration Committee, an official replica of the Tony Award medallion upon such winner's execution and delivery to the Tony Awards Administration Committee of a Tony Award Medallion Receipt agreement in the form of Exhibit B to these Rules.

(g) "Tony Honors for Excellence in the Theatre" may be given in the discretion of the Tony Awards Administration Committee. Such Honors shall be granted only if the Tony Awards Administration Committee, after applying objective and fair standards, determines that the candidate has made contributions qualifying for "excellence in the theatre." Anyone may, not later than 30 days prior to the Eligibility Date, recommend in writing a candidate for Tony Honors consideration by the Tony Awards Administration Committee.

(h) Each recipient of "Tony Honors for Excellence in the

Theatre", and no other person, will be entitled to receive from the Tony Awards Administration Committee, an official Tony Honors medallion upon such recipient's execution and delivery to the Tony Awards Administration Committee of a Tony Honors Medallion Receipt Agreement in the form of Exhibit C to these Rules.

(i) Anything in these Rules to the contrary notwithstanding, no "Special Tony Award" may be given unless specifically requested by a member of the Tony Awards Administration Committee in writing to the other members of the Tony Awards Administration Committee, which writing is delivered, together with all supporting material, no later than the Submission Date.

5. SELECTION OF WINNERS OF REGULAR AWARDS
    (a) *The Nominating Committee.*

i) The *"Nominating Committee"* shall consist of no fewer than 15 and no more than 30 persons appointed by the Tony Awards Administration Committee as provided herein. Of the persons so appointed, and who accept such appointment, for the 1997-98 theatrical season, they shall be divided randomly (by lot) into three classes of as nearly equal number as possible (and in no event fewer than five members of any one class) to serve for one-, two- and three-season terms commencing with the beginning of such season.* The Nominating Committee shall be selected so as to assure that each eligible production and performer shall have been seen by as many members as possible. Members of the Nominating Committee shall make every effort to attend a preview or opening night performance. Expenses shall not be provided or reimbursed to members of the Nominating Committee.

ii) The Nominating Committee shall meet, following the Eligibility Date of the current season, on the date designated by the Tony Awards Administration Committee for the purpose of determining the nominees for Tony Awards for such season. At such meeting, the Nominating Committee shall be given a separate ballot for each category containing a list compiled by the Tony Awards Administration Committee of the eligible candidates for nomination and the number of nominees in such category. The Nominating Committee shall be permitted to discuss the qualifications of the eligible candidates for all cate-

---

For each of season following the 1996–97 theatrical season, the intent of is that the members of at least one class rotate off the committee for at least one season, so that each season the committee shall include at least five members who did not serve on the committee for the immediately preceding season.

gories for up to a maximum of two hours immediately prior to voting to determine all nominations, but shall not, in any event, take any "straw" poll or otherwise informally determine or attempt to determine the likely voting results. At the conclusion of such two-hour open discussion period, each member of the Nominating Committee shall cast his/her secret ballot for the best candidates of the season in all categories (as provided herein) and such ballot shall be collected by a representative of the Accounting Firm. The Nominating Committee shall, consistent with these Rules, make its nominations solely based on the standard of the best in the current season. The vote of each member of the Nominating Committee must be based on the ballot (and the list included therein). The Nominating Committee shall await the tally of their voting without further discussion. Any ties shall be resolved as provided in these Rules. Neither write-in votes nor proxies shall be permitted. The Accounting Firm shall tabulate the votes of the Nominating Committee and shall announce the nominees to the members of the Nominating Committee and the Tony Awards Administration Committee only following the determination of all nominees in all categories (and shall not disclose or announce any nominees, formally or informally, prior to such time). The actual number of votes received by those eligible (including the nominees) in each category shall not be disclosed by the Accounting Firm to anyone on the Tony Awards Administration Committee, the Nominating Committee or to any other person or entity.

iii) Each member of the Nominating Committee shall be entitled to cast one, and only one, vote for each eligible candidate on such person's ballot, and no more votes than the number of nominees prescribed by the Tony Awards Administration Committee on the ballot (i.e., if there are to be four nominees, one vote each for four eligible candidates as nominees) in each category. The nominees in each category shall be the eligible candidates that receive the most votes up to the number of prescribed nominees (e.g., if there are to be four nominees, then the nominees shall be the candidate that receives the most votes, the candidate that receives the next-most votes, the candidate that receives the third-highest number of votes and the candidate that receives the fourth-highest number of votes). No member of the Nominating Committee may abstain in any category or vote for fewer than the prescribed number of nominees in any category. In the event the vote of the Nominating Committee results in a tie that would otherwise necessitate more than the prescribed number of nominees in a category, said tie shall be broken in the manner described in paragraph 5(b) of these Rules. Once the categories have been established by the Tony Awards Administration Committee, the Nominating Committee shall have no power to eliminate a category.

(b) *Tie-Breaking for Nominees*. Upon determining the existence of a tie requiring a tie-breaking vote, the Accounting Firm shall immediately submit such tied candidates to the Nominating Committee for an immediate tie-breaking vote as provided herein. Upon making any such submission for re-voting to break a tie, no announcement or disclosure shall be made as to any of the nominees in such category or in any other category. If there are only two candidates tied *and* if there are an even number of members of the Nominating Committee present, then the members of the Nominating Committee shall draw lots to determine which of them shall not vote to break the tie. Voting to break a tie among three or more candidates shall be on a cumulative (i.e., "weighted") basis. For example, if there are three tied candidates, each member of the Nominating Committee shall give one of such candidates three votes, one such candidate two votes and one such candidate one vote, in order of preference, with the more preferred receiving more votes. The weight will depend solely on the discretion of the member of the Nominating Committee in each case; provided, that each member of the Nominating Committee shall be required to cast all the votes. The Accounting Firm shall determine which candidate(s) among those tied received the highest number of votes in the heaviest weighting category (e.g., if three candidates are tied, the "3" votes, and so on). The candidate(s) with the highest number of such votes among those tied shall receive the nomination(s), until there is no longer a tie necessitating more than the prescribed number of nominees. If any of those tied have the same number of such votes (e.g., if there are three candidates, the same number of "3" votes), the Accounting Firm shall then determine which of said candidates received the highest number of votes in the second heaviest weighing category (e.g., if there are three candidates, the "2" votes, and so on), in which event the candidate with the highest number of such votes shall receive the nomination.

(c) *Persons Eligible to Vote*. The persons eligible to vote for the purpose of determining winners of the Tony Awards shall be the members of the governing boards of the following organizations:

1. Actors' Equity Association
2. The Dramatists Guild
3. Society of Stage Directors & Choreographers
4. United Scenic Artists

and those persons whose names appear on the Designated Press Performances and First Night List, up to 45 persons from among the Board of Directors and the Advisory Board of the Wing (as designated by the Wing), the Voting Members of The League (in accordance with The League's requirements, as confirmed by The League), no more than 15 members of the Theatrical Council of the Casting Society of America designated by such Council and no more than 15 members of the current governing board (exclusive of alternates or members emeritus) of the Association of Theatrical Press Agents and Managers designated by such Association; provided, that in no event shall there be any duplication (i.e., no person shall be entitled to more than one vote as a result of such person's qualification or inclusion in more than one of the foregoing categories). Employees (other than the Executive Director or equivalent) of any of the foregoing organizations shall not be eligible to vote for the winners of the Tony Awards. The Tony Awards Administration Committee shall have the right, in its discretion, to remove any person from eligibility to vote in the current season in the event said person has not exercised his/her right to vote in the prior season or who violates any rule herein.

(d) *Ballots of Persons Eligible to Vote.* No ballot shall be counted unless the voter casting it has certified to the Tony Awards Administration Committee that, with respect to each category in which the voter has voted, the voter has seen a performance of each production which has been nominated for an Award and a performance by each performer who has been nominated in the production with respect to which such performer has been nominated. The ballot may provide that marking and returning it constitutes such a certification. Write-in votes shall not be permitted.

(e) *Identity of Eligible Voters.* As complete a list as possible of all such eligible voters shall be sent to each producer prior to the first paid public performance of the production.

(f) *Accounting Firm.* The firm of independent certified public accountants selected by the Tony Awards Management Committee (the "*Accounting Firm*") shall mail a ballot containing the names of the nominees to each eligible voter at least 14 days prior to the date on which the Tony Awards are to be presented for such season, with a request to deliver completed ballots directly to the

Accounting Firm. Such firm shall count and tabulate those ballots received at least 52 hours prior to the commencement of the formal presentation of the Tony Awards for such season and shall certify the winners to the Tony Awards Administration Committee.

(g)*Selection of Winners.* The Tony Award shall be given to the person, production or element thereof that is voted the best in the current season for each eligible category, and votes are to be cast according to that standard. The winner in each category shall be the nominee in that category receiving the highest number of votes. No tabulation of the numbers of votes for each nominee shall be disclosed to the Tony Awards Administration Committee or Nominating Committee or to any other person or entity, and the names of the winners shall not be similarly disclosed until the presentation of the Awards.

EXHIBIT A
Eligible Theatres

Ambassador
215 West 49 Street

Brooks Atkinson
256 West 47 Street

Ethel Barrymore
243 West 47 Street

Vivian Beaumont
150 West 65 Street

Martin Beck
302 West 45 Street

Belasco
111 West 44 Street

Booth
222 West 45 Street

Broadhurst
235 West 44 Street

Broadway
1681 Broadway

Circle in the Square
1633 Broadway

Cort
138 West 48 Street

Ford Centre for
the Performing Arts
213 West 42 Street

Gershwin
1633 Broadway

John Golden
252 West 45 Street

*Helen Hayes
240 West 44 Street

Imperial
249 West 45 Street

Walter Kerr
219 West 48 Street

Longacre
220 West 48 Street

Lunt-Fontanne
205 West 46 Street

Lyceum
149 West 45 Street

Majestic
245 West 44 Street

Marquis
Marriott Hotel
1535 Broadway

Henry Miller
124 West 43 Street

Minskoff
200 West 45 Street

Music Box
239 West 45 Street

Nederlander
208 West 41 Street

New Amsterdam
214 West 42 Street

Eugene O'Neill
230 West 49 Street

Palace
1564 Broadway

Plymouth
236 West 45 Street

Richard Rodgers
226 West 46 Street

Royale
242 West 45 Street

St. James
246 West 44 Street

Selwyn
West 42nd Street

Shubert
225 West 44 Street

Neil Simon
250 West 52 Street

*Stage Right
1530 Broadway

Studio 54
254 W. 54 Street

Virginia
245 West 52 Street

Winter Garden
1634 Broadway

* These theatres were deemed "eligible Broadway theatres" prior to the amendment of the rule (effective for the 1989-90 Season) which increased the minimum seating requirement from 499 to 500 and thus, each of theatres are "grandfathered" and continue to be deemed eligible provided they do not reduce their seating capacity to below the number of seats such theatre made available to the public on June 1, 1989.

EXHIBIT B
Tony Award® *Medallion Receipt Agreement*

Tony Award Productions
226 West 47th Street
New York, New York 10036

Re: **Tony Award Medallion for (Category to be filled in) / 2000-01 Season**

Ladies and Gentlemen:

The undersigned hereby acknowledges receipt from you of a replica (the "Replica") of the medallion commonly known as the Tony Award® Medallion which commemorates the referenced Tony Award®. The undersigned acknowledges that receipt of the Replica does not entitle the undersigned to any right whatsoever in the copyright of such medallion (or any trade or service mark represented thereby). The undersigned further acknowledges that the undersigned will not be entitled to any additional Replicas of such medallion and that a replacement therefore will only be provided upon demonstration, satisfactory to you, that the Replica has been lost, stolen or destroyed.

The undersigned expressly acknowledges that the distribution of the Replica through commercial channels would irreparably cause incalculable harm to the integrity of the Tony Awards®. In consideration of both the foregoing and your delivering the Replica to the undersigned, the undersigned agrees to comply with all your rules and regulations respecting its use and not to sell or otherwise dispose of it, nor permit it to be sold or disposed of by operation of law or otherwise, without first offering to sell it to Tony Award Productions for the sum of $10.00. You will have 60 days after any such offer is made in which to accept it. Any such offer must be made expressly in writing delivered to Tony Award Productions.

This agreement shall be binding not only on the undersigned, but also on the heirs, legatees, personal representatives, executors, administrators, estate successors and assigns of the undersigned, if a natural person, and the partners, members, stockholders, directors, officers, employees and agents of the undersigned, if other than a natural person. If the undersigned is a natural person, the designees, heirs, legatees and personal representative of the undersigned may acquire title to the Replica, if it becomes part of the undersigned's estate, subject to the terms of this agreement.

This agreement shall be governed by and construed in accordance with laws of the State of New York applicable to contracts made and performed wholly therein. The undersigned hereby consent to the exclusive jurisdiction of the courts of the State of New York and the United States courts located in the State of New York, in connection with any lawsuit, action or proceeding arising out of, or related to, this agreement, and agrees to reimburse Tony Award Productions for any and all costs and expenses (including without limitation, attorneys' fees and disbursements) in enforcing the terms hereof in any action or proceeding.

SIGNATURE OF RECIPIENT

DATED

EXHIBIT C
Tony Honors Medallion Receipt Agreement

Tony Award Productions
226 West 47th Street
New York, New York 10036

Re: **Tony Honors Medallion for (Category to be filled in) /
2000-01 Season**

Ladies and Gentlemen:

The undersigned hereby acknowledges receipt from you of a replica (the "Replica") of the medallion commonly known as the Tony Honors Medallion which commemorates the referenced Tony Honor. The undersigned acknowledges that receipt of the Replica does not entitle the undersigned to any right whatsoever in the copyright of such medallion (or any trade or service mark represented thereby). The undersigned further acknowledges that the undersigned will not be entitled to any additional Replicas of such medallion and that a replacement therefore will only be provided upon demonstration, satisfactory to you, that the Replica has been lost, stolen or destroyed.

The undersigned expressly acknowledges that the distribution of the Replica through commercial channels would irreparably cause incalculable harm to the integrity of the Tony Awards®. In consideration of both the foregoing and your delivering the Replica to the undersigned, the undersigned agrees to comply with all your rules and regulations respecting its use and not to sell or otherwise dispose of it, nor permit it to be sold or disposed of by operation of law or otherwise, without first offering to sell it to Tony Award Productions for the sum of $10.00. You will have 60 days after any such offer is made in which to accept it. Any such offer must be made expressly in writing delivered to Tony Award Productions.

This agreement shall be binding not only on the undersigned, but also on the heirs, legatees, personal representatives, executors, administrators, estate successors and assigns of the undersigned, if a natural person, and the partners, members, stockholders, directors, officers, employees and agents of the undersigned, if other than a natural person. If the undersigned is a natural person, the designees, heirs, legatees and personal representative of the undersigned may acquire title to the Replica, if it becomes part of the undersigned's estate, subject to the terms of this agreement.

This agreement shall be governed by and construed in accordance with laws of the State of New York applicable to contracts made and performed wholly therein. The undersigend hereby consent to the exclusive jurisdiction of the courts of the State of New York and the United States courts located in the State of New York, in connection with any lawsuit, action or proceeding arising out of, or related to, this agreement, and agrees to reimburse Tony Award Productions for any and all costs and expenses (including without limitation, attorneys' fees and disbursements) in enforcing the terms hereof in any action or proceeding.

___

SIGNATURE OF RECIPIENT

___

DATED

Index

Page numbers in boldface indicate the location of a Tony Award winner.

Index

Index

Index

Index

The Tony Award®

Index

Index

Index

6689